C-1066   CAREER EXAMINATION SERIES

This is your
PASSBOOK for...

Trackman (Track Worker)

Test Preparation Study Guide
Questions & Answers

COPYRIGHT NOTICE

This book is SOLELY intended for, is sold ONLY to, and its use is RESTRICTED to individual, bona fide applicants or candidates who qualify by virtue of having seriously filed applications for appropriate license, certificate, professional and/or promotional advancement, higher school matriculation, scholarship, or other legitimate requirements of education and/or governmental authorities.

This book is NOT intended for use, class instruction, tutoring, training, duplication, copying, reprinting, excerption, or adaptation, etc., by:

1) Other publishers
2) Proprietors and/or Instructors of "Coaching" and/or Preparatory Courses
3) Personnel and/or Training Divisions of commercial, industrial, and governmental organizations
4) Schools, colleges, or universities and/or their departments and staffs, including teachers and other personnel
5) Testing Agencies or Bureaus
6) Study groups which seek by the purchase of a single volume to copy and/or duplicate and/or adapt this material for use by the group as a whole without having purchased individual volumes for each of the members of the group
7) Et al.

Such persons would be in violation of appropriate Federal and State statutes.

PROVISION OF LICENSING AGREEMENTS – Recognized educational, commercial, industrial, and governmental institutions and organizations, and others legitimately engaged in educational pursuits, including training, testing, and measurement activities, may address request for a licensing agreement to the copyright owners, who will determine whether, and under what conditions, including fees and charges, the materials in this book may be used them. In other words, a licensing facility exists for the legitimate use of the material in this book on other than an individual basis. However, it is asseverated and affirmed here that the material in this book CANNOT be used without the receipt of the express permission of such a licensing agreement from the Publishers. Inquiries re licensing should be addressed to the company, attention rights and permissions department.

All rights reserved, including the right of reproduction in whole or in part, in any form or by any means, electronic or mechanical, including photocopying, recording, or by any information storage and retrieval system, without permission in writing from the Publisher.

Copyright © 2024 by
National Learning Corporation

212 Michael Drive, Syosset, NY 11791
(516) 921-8888 • www.passbooks.com
E-mail: info@passbooks.com

PUBLISHED IN THE UNITED STATES OF AMERICA

PASSBOOK® SERIES

THE *PASSBOOK® SERIES* has been created to prepare applicants and candidates for the ultimate academic battlefield – the examination room.

At some time in our lives, each and every one of us may be required to take an examination – for validation, matriculation, admission, qualification, registration, certification, or licensure.

Based on the assumption that every applicant or candidate has met the basic formal educational standards, has taken the required number of courses, and read the necessary texts, the *PASSBOOK® SERIES* furnishes the one special preparation which may assure passing with confidence, instead of failing with insecurity. Examination questions – together with answers – are furnished as the basic vehicle for study so that the mysteries of the examination and its compounding difficulties may be eliminated or diminished by a sure method.

This book is meant to help you pass your examination provided that you qualify and are serious in your objective.

The entire field is reviewed through the huge store of content information which is succinctly presented through a provocative and challenging approach – the question-and-answer method.

A climate of success is established by furnishing the correct answers at the end of each test.

You soon learn to recognize types of questions, forms of questions, and patterns of questioning. You may even begin to anticipate expected outcomes.

You perceive that many questions are repeated or adapted so that you can gain acute insights, which may enable you to score many sure points.

You learn how to confront new questions, or types of questions, and to attack them confidently and work out the correct answers.

You note objectives and emphases, and recognize pitfalls and dangers, so that you may make positive educational adjustments.

Moreover, you are kept fully informed in relation to new concepts, methods, practices, and directions in the field.

You discover that you are actually taking the examination all the time: you are preparing for the examination by "taking" an examination, not by reading extraneous and/or supererogatory textbooks.

In short, this PASSBOOK®, used directedly, should be an important factor in helping you to pass your test.

TRACKMAN (TRACK WORKER)

DUTIES:
Track Workers, under supervision, maintain, install, inspect, test, alter, and repair the track and roadway in subway and elevated service under operating conditions. This includes, but is not limited to, the maintenance, installation, inspection, testing, alteration and repair of rails, frogs, switches, ties, plates and insulated joints, and their related adjusting, tamping, welding, grinding, greasing and cleaning. Track Workers perform related work.

THE TEST
The competitive multiple-choice test may include questions that require the use of any of the following abilities:

- **Written Comprehension** — The ability to understand written sentences or paragraphs. Example: Reading and understanding a safety bulletin.
- **Written Expression** — The ability to use English words or sentences in writing so others will understand. Example: Writing an incident report.
- **Deductive Reasoning** — The ability to apply general rules to specific problems to come up with logical answers. It involves deciding if an answer makes sense. Example: Following the rules for operating equipment.
- **Inductive Reasoning** — The ability to combine separate pieces of information, or specific answers to problems to form general rules or conclusions. It includes coming up with a logical explanation for why a series of unrelated events occur together. Example: Determining an unsafe condition based on different issues observed on the track.
- **Information Ordering** — The ability to follow correctly a rule or set of rules to arrange things or actions in a certain order. The rule or sets of rules used must be given. The things or actions to be put in order can include numbers, letters, words, pictures, procedures, sentences, and mathematical or logical operations. Example: Laying out track material in the correct order when installing track.
- **Memorization** — The ability to remember information, such as words, numbers, pictures, and procedures. Example: Remembering instructions given by a supervisor.
- **Problem Sensitivity** — The ability to tell when something is wrong or likely to go wrong. It includes being able to identify the whole problem as well as elements of the problem. Example: Recognizing when a track is not installed correctly.
- **Visualization** — The ability to imagine how something will look after it is moved around or when its parts are moved or rearranged. Example: Determining how an obstruction along the trackway will look when you are standing on the opposite side of it.
- **Spatial Orientation** — The ability to tell where you are in relation to the location of some object or to tell where the object is in relation to you. Example: Determining track configurations based on diagrams.
- **Mechanical Aptitude** — The ability to understand and apply mechanical concepts and principles to solve problems. Example: Choosing the appropriate screwdriver to turn a certain screw head.
- **Dial/Gauge Reading** — The ability to monitor gauges, dials, or other indicators to ensure that a piece of equipment or machine is working correctly. Example: Reading switch inspection gauges.
- **Perceptual Speed** — The ability to quickly and accurately compare similarities and differences among sets of letters, numbers, objects, pictures, or patterns. Example: Navigating the trackway using track marker signs.

HOW TO TAKE A TEST

I. YOU MUST PASS AN EXAMINATION

A. WHAT EVERY CANDIDATE SHOULD KNOW

Examination applicants often ask us for help in preparing for the written test. What can I study in advance? What kinds of questions will be asked? How will the test be given? How will the papers be graded?

As an applicant for a civil service examination, you may be wondering about some of these things. Our purpose here is to suggest effective methods of advance study and to describe civil service examinations.

Your chances for success on this examination can be increased if you know how to prepare. Those "pre-examination jitters" can be reduced if you know what to expect. You can even experience an adventure in good citizenship if you know why civil service exams are given.

B. WHY ARE CIVIL SERVICE EXAMINATIONS GIVEN?

Civil service examinations are important to you in two ways. As a citizen, you want public jobs filled by employees who know how to do their work. As a job seeker, you want a fair chance to compete for that job on an equal footing with other candidates. The best-known means of accomplishing this two-fold goal is the competitive examination.

Exams are widely publicized throughout the nation. They may be administered for jobs in federal, state, city, municipal, town or village governments or agencies.

Any citizen may apply, with some limitations, such as the age or residence of applicants. Your experience and education may be reviewed to see whether you meet the requirements for the particular examination. When these requirements exist, they are reasonable and applied consistently to all applicants. Thus, a competitive examination may cause you some uneasiness now, but it is your privilege and safeguard.

C. HOW ARE CIVIL SERVICE EXAMS DEVELOPED?

Examinations are carefully written by trained technicians who are specialists in the field known as "psychological measurement," in consultation with recognized authorities in the field of work that the test will cover. These experts recommend the subject matter areas or skills to be tested; only those knowledges or skills important to your success on the job are included. The most reliable books and source materials available are used as references. Together, the experts and technicians judge the difficulty level of the questions.

Test technicians know how to phrase questions so that the problem is clearly stated. Their ethics do not permit "trick" or "catch" questions. Questions may have been tried out on sample groups, or subjected to statistical analysis, to determine their usefulness.

Written tests are often used in combination with performance tests, ratings of training and experience, and oral interviews. All of these measures combine to form the best-known means of finding the right person for the right job.

II. HOW TO PASS THE WRITTEN TEST

A. NATURE OF THE EXAMINATION

To prepare intelligently for civil service examinations, you should know how they differ from school examinations you have taken. In school you were assigned certain definite pages to read or subjects to cover. The examination questions were quite detailed and usually emphasized memory. Civil service exams, on the other hand, try to discover your present ability to perform the duties of a position, plus your potentiality to learn these duties. In other words, a civil service exam attempts to predict how successful you will be. Questions cover such a broad area that they cannot be as minute and detailed as school exam questions.

In the public service similar kinds of work, or positions, are grouped together in one "class." This process is known as *position-classification*. All the positions in a class are paid according to the salary range for that class. One class title covers all of these positions, and they are all tested by the same examination.

B. FOUR BASIC STEPS

1) Study the announcement

How, then, can you know what subjects to study? Our best answer is: "Learn as much as possible about the class of positions for which you've applied." The exam will test the knowledge, skills and abilities needed to do the work.

Your most valuable source of information about the position you want is the official exam announcement. This announcement lists the training and experience qualifications. Check these standards and apply only if you come reasonably close to meeting them.

The brief description of the position in the examination announcement offers some clues to the subjects which will be tested. Think about the job itself. Review the duties in your mind. Can you perform them, or are there some in which you are rusty? Fill in the blank spots in your preparation.

Many jurisdictions preview the written test in the exam announcement by including a section called "Knowledge and Abilities Required," "Scope of the Examination," or some similar heading. Here you will find out specifically what fields will be tested.

2) Review your own background

Once you learn in general what the position is all about, and what you need to know to do the work, ask yourself which subjects you already know fairly well and which need improvement. You may wonder whether to concentrate on improving your strong areas or on building some background in your fields of weakness. When the announcement has specified "some knowledge" or "considerable knowledge," or has used adjectives like "beginning principles of…" or "advanced … methods," you can get a clue as to the number and difficulty of questions to be asked in any given field. More questions, and hence broader coverage, would be included for those subjects which are more important in the work. Now weigh your strengths and weaknesses against the job requirements and prepare accordingly.

3) Determine the level of the position

Another way to tell how intensively you should prepare is to understand the level of the job for which you are applying. Is it the entering level? In other words, is this the position in which beginners in a field of work are hired? Or is it an intermediate or advanced level? Sometimes this is indicated by such words as "Junior" or "Senior" in the class title. Other jurisdictions use Roman numerals to designate the level – Clerk I, Clerk II, for example. The word "Supervisor" sometimes appears in the title. If the level is not indicated by the title, check the description of duties. Will you be working under very close supervision, or will you have responsibility for independent decisions in this work?

4) Choose appropriate study materials

Now that you know the subjects to be examined and the relative amount of each subject to be covered, you can choose suitable study materials. For beginning level jobs, or even advanced ones, if you have a pronounced weakness in some aspect of your training, read a modern, standard textbook in that field. Be sure it is up to date and has general coverage. Such books are normally available at your library, and the librarian will be glad to help you locate one. For entry-level positions, questions of appropriate difficulty are chosen – neither highly advanced questions, nor those too simple. Such questions require careful thought but not advanced training.

If the position for which you are applying is technical or advanced, you will read more advanced, specialized material. If you are already familiar with the basic principles of your field, elementary textbooks would waste your time. Concentrate on advanced textbooks and technical periodicals. Think through the concepts and review difficult problems in your field.

These are all general sources. You can get more ideas on your own initiative, following these leads. For example, training manuals and publications of the government agency which employs workers in your field can be useful, particularly for technical and professional positions. A letter or visit to the government department involved may result in more specific study suggestions, and certainly will provide you with a more definite idea of the exact nature of the position you are seeking.

III. KINDS OF TESTS

Tests are used for purposes other than measuring knowledge and ability to perform specified duties. For some positions, it is equally important to test ability to make adjustments to new situations or to profit from training. In others, basic mental abilities not dependent on information are essential. Questions which test these things may not appear as pertinent to the duties of the position as those which test for knowledge and information. Yet they are often highly important parts of a fair examination. For very general questions, it is almost impossible to help you direct your study efforts. What we can do is to point out some of the more common of these general abilities needed in public service positions and describe some typical questions.

1) General information

Broad, general information has been found useful for predicting job success in some kinds of work. This is tested in a variety of ways, from vocabulary lists to questions about current events. Basic background in some field of work, such as sociology or economics, may be sampled in a group of questions. Often these are principles which have become familiar to most persons through exposure rather than through formal training. It is difficult to advise you how to study for these questions; being alert to the world around you is our best suggestion.

2) Verbal ability

An example of an ability needed in many positions is verbal or language ability. Verbal ability is, in brief, the ability to use and understand words. Vocabulary and grammar tests are typical measures of this ability. Reading comprehension or paragraph interpretation questions are common in many kinds of civil service tests. You are given a paragraph of written material and asked to find its central meaning.

3) Numerical ability

Number skills can be tested by the familiar arithmetic problem, by checking paired lists of numbers to see which are alike and which are different, or by interpreting charts and graphs. In the latter test, a graph may be printed in the test booklet which you are asked to use as the basis for answering questions.

4) Observation

A popular test for law-enforcement positions is the observation test. A picture is shown to you for several minutes, then taken away. Questions about the picture test your ability to observe both details and larger elements.

5) Following directions

In many positions in the public service, the employee must be able to carry out written instructions dependably and accurately. You may be given a chart with several columns, each column listing a variety of information. The questions require you to carry out directions involving the information given in the chart.

6) Skills and aptitudes

Performance tests effectively measure some manual skills and aptitudes. When the skill is one in which you are trained, such as typing or shorthand, you can practice. These tests are often very much like those given in business school or high school courses. For many of the other skills and aptitudes, however, no short-time preparation can be made. Skills and abilities natural to you or that you have developed throughout your lifetime are being tested.

Many of the general questions just described provide all the data needed to answer the questions and ask you to use your reasoning ability to find the answers. Your best preparation for these tests, as well as for tests of facts and ideas, is to be at your physical and mental best. You, no doubt, have your own methods of getting into an exam-taking mood and keeping "in shape." The next section lists some ideas on this subject.

IV. KINDS OF QUESTIONS

Only rarely is the "essay" question, which you answer in narrative form, used in civil service tests. Civil service tests are usually of the short-answer type. Full instructions for answering these questions will be given to you at the examination. But in case this is your first experience with short-answer questions and separate answer sheets, here is what you need to know:

1) **Multiple-choice Questions**

Most popular of the short-answer questions is the "multiple choice" or "best answer" question. It can be used, for example, to test for factual knowledge, ability to solve problems or judgment in meeting situations found at work.

A multiple-choice question is normally one of three types—
- It can begin with an incomplete statement followed by several possible endings. You are to find the one ending which *best* completes the statement, although some of the others may not be entirely wrong.
- It can also be a complete statement in the form of a question which is answered by choosing one of the statements listed.

- It can be in the form of a problem – again you select the best answer.

Here is an example of a multiple-choice question with a discussion which should give you some clues as to the method for choosing the right answer:

When an employee has a complaint about his assignment, the action which will *best* help him overcome his difficulty is to
   A. discuss his difficulty with his coworkers
   B. take the problem to the head of the organization
   C. take the problem to the person who gave him the assignment
   D. say nothing to anyone about his complaint

In answering this question, you should study each of the choices to find which is best. Consider choice "A" – Certainly an employee may discuss his complaint with fellow employees, but no change or improvement can result, and the complaint remains unresolved. Choice "B" is a poor choice since the head of the organization probably does not know what assignment you have been given, and taking your problem to him is known as "going over the head" of the supervisor. The supervisor, or person who made the assignment, is the person who can clarify it or correct any injustice. Choice "C" is, therefore, correct. To say nothing, as in choice "D," is unwise. Supervisors have and interest in knowing the problems employees are facing, and the employee is seeking a solution to his problem.

2) True/False Questions

The "true/false" or "right/wrong" form of question is sometimes used. Here a complete statement is given. Your job is to decide whether the statement is right or wrong.

SAMPLE: A roaming cell-phone call to a nearby city costs less than a non-roaming call to a distant city.

This statement is wrong, or false, since roaming calls are more expensive.
This is not a complete list of all possible question forms, although most of the others are variations of these common types. You will always get complete directions for answering questions. Be sure you understand *how* to mark your answers – ask questions until you do.

V. RECORDING YOUR ANSWERS

Computer terminals are used more and more today for many different kinds of exams.
For an examination with very few applicants, you may be told to record your answers in the test booklet itself. Separate answer sheets are much more common. If this separate answer sheet is to be scored by machine – and this is often the case – it is highly important that you mark your answers correctly in order to get credit.
An electronic scoring machine is often used in civil service offices because of the speed with which papers can be scored. Machine-scored answer sheets must be marked with a pencil, which will be given to you. This pencil has a high graphite content which responds to the electronic scoring machine. As a matter of fact, stray dots may register as answers, so do not let your pencil rest on the answer sheet while you are pondering the correct answer. Also, if your pencil lead breaks or is otherwise defective, ask for another.

Since the answer sheet will be dropped in a slot in the scoring machine, be careful not to bend the corners or get the paper crumpled.

The answer sheet normally has five vertical columns of numbers, with 30 numbers to a column. These numbers correspond to the question numbers in your test booklet. After each number, going across the page are four or five pairs of dotted lines. These short dotted lines have small letters or numbers above them. The first two pairs may also have a "T" or "F" above the letters. This indicates that the first two pairs only are to be used if the questions are of the true-false type. If the questions are multiple choice, disregard the "T" and "F" and pay attention only to the small letters or numbers.

Answer your questions in the manner of the sample that follows:

32. The largest city in the United States is
   A. Washington, D.C.
   B. New York City
   C. Chicago
   D. Detroit
   E. San Francisco

1) Choose the answer you think is best. (New York City is the largest, so "B" is correct.)
2) Find the row of dotted lines numbered the same as the question you are answering. (Find row number 32)
3) Find the pair of dotted lines corresponding to the answer. (Find the pair of lines under the mark "B.")
4) Make a solid black mark between the dotted lines.

VI. BEFORE THE TEST

Common sense will help you find procedures to follow to get ready for an examination. Too many of us, however, overlook these sensible measures. Indeed, nervousness and fatigue have been found to be the most serious reasons why applicants fail to do their best on civil service tests. Here is a list of reminders:

- Begin your preparation early – Don't wait until the last minute to go scurrying around for books and materials or to find out what the position is all about.
- Prepare continuously – An hour a night for a week is better than an all-night cram session. This has been definitely established. What is more, a night a week for a month will return better dividends than crowding your study into a shorter period of time.
- Locate the place of the exam – You have been sent a notice telling you when and where to report for the examination. If the location is in a different town or otherwise unfamiliar to you, it would be well to inquire the best route and learn something about the building.
- Relax the night before the test – Allow your mind to rest. Do not study at all that night. Plan some mild recreation or diversion; then go to bed early and get a good night's sleep.
- Get up early enough to make a leisurely trip to the place for the test – This way unforeseen events, traffic snarls, unfamiliar buildings, etc. will not upset you.
- Dress comfortably – A written test is not a fashion show. You will be known by number and not by name, so wear something comfortable.

- Leave excess paraphernalia at home – Shopping bags and odd bundles will get in your way. You need bring only the items mentioned in the official notice you received; usually everything you need is provided. Do not bring reference books to the exam. They will only confuse those last minutes and be taken away from you when in the test room.
- Arrive somewhat ahead of time – If because of transportation schedules you must get there very early, bring a newspaper or magazine to take your mind off yourself while waiting.
- Locate the examination room – When you have found the proper room, you will be directed to the seat or part of the room where you will sit. Sometimes you are given a sheet of instructions to read while you are waiting. Do not fill out any forms until you are told to do so; just read them and be prepared.
- Relax and prepare to listen to the instructions
- If you have any physical problem that may keep you from doing your best, be sure to tell the test administrator. If you are sick or in poor health, you really cannot do your best on the exam. You can come back and take the test some other time.

VII. AT THE TEST

The day of the test is here and you have the test booklet in your hand. The temptation to get going is very strong. Caution! There is more to success than knowing the right answers. You must know how to identify your papers and understand variations in the type of short-answer question used in this particular examination. Follow these suggestions for maximum results from your efforts:

1) Cooperate with the monitor

The test administrator has a duty to create a situation in which you can be as much at ease as possible. He will give instructions, tell you when to begin, check to see that you are marking your answer sheet correctly, and so on. He is not there to guard you, although he will see that your competitors do not take unfair advantage. He wants to help you do your best.

2) Listen to all instructions

Don't jump the gun! Wait until you understand all directions. In most civil service tests you get more time than you need to answer the questions. So don't be in a hurry. Read each word of instructions until you clearly understand the meaning. Study the examples, listen to all announcements and follow directions. Ask questions if you do not understand what to do.

3) Identify your papers

Civil service exams are usually identified by number only. You will be assigned a number; you must not put your name on your test papers. Be sure to copy your number correctly. Since more than one exam may be given, copy your exact examination title.

4) Plan your time

Unless you are told that a test is a "speed" or "rate of work" test, speed itself is usually not important. Time enough to answer all the questions will be provided, but this does not mean that you have all day. An overall time limit has been set. Divide the total time (in minutes) by the number of questions to determine the approximate time you have for each question.

5) Do not linger over difficult questions

If you come across a difficult question, mark it with a paper clip (useful to have along) and come back to it when you have been through the booklet. One caution if you do this – be sure to skip a number on your answer sheet as well. Check often to be sure that you have not lost your place and that you are marking in the row numbered the same as the question you are answering.

6) Read the questions

Be sure you know what the question asks! Many capable people are unsuccessful because they failed to *read* the questions correctly.

7) Answer all questions

Unless you have been instructed that a penalty will be deducted for incorrect answers, it is better to guess than to omit a question.

8) Speed tests

It is often better NOT to guess on speed tests. It has been found that on timed tests people are tempted to spend the last few seconds before time is called in marking answers at random – without even reading them – in the hope of picking up a few extra points. To discourage this practice, the instructions may warn you that your score will be "corrected" for guessing. That is, a penalty will be applied. The incorrect answers will be deducted from the correct ones, or some other penalty formula will be used.

9) Review your answers

If you finish before time is called, go back to the questions you guessed or omitted to give them further thought. Review other answers if you have time.

10) Return your test materials

If you are ready to leave before others have finished or time is called, take ALL your materials to the monitor and leave quietly. Never take any test material with you. The monitor can discover whose papers are not complete, and taking a test booklet may be grounds for disqualification.

VIII. EXAMINATION TECHNIQUES

1) Read the general instructions carefully. These are usually printed on the first page of the exam booklet. As a rule, these instructions refer to the timing of the examination; the fact that you should not start work until the signal and must stop work at a signal, etc. If there are any *special* instructions, such as a choice of questions to be answered, make sure that you note this instruction carefully.

2) When you are ready to start work on the examination, that is as soon as the signal has been given, read the instructions to each question booklet, underline any key words or phrases, such as *least, best, outline, describe* and the like. In this way you will tend to answer as requested rather than discover on reviewing your paper that you *listed without describing*, that you selected the *worst* choice rather than the *best* choice, etc.

3) If the examination is of the objective or multiple-choice type – that is, each question will also give a series of possible answers: A, B, C or D, and you are called upon to select the best answer and write the letter next to that answer on your answer paper – it is advisable to start answering each question in turn. There may be anywhere from 50 to 100 such questions in the three or four hours allotted and you can see how much time would be taken if you read through all the questions before beginning to answer any. Furthermore, if you come across a question or group of questions which you know would be difficult to answer, it would undoubtedly affect your handling of all the other questions.

4) If the examination is of the essay type and contains but a few questions, it is a moot point as to whether you should read all the questions before starting to answer any one. Of course, if you are given a choice – say five out of seven and the like – then it is essential to read all the questions so you can eliminate the two that are most difficult. If, however, you are asked to answer all the questions, there may be danger in trying to answer the easiest one first because you may find that you will spend too much time on it. The best technique is to answer the first question, then proceed to the second, etc.

5) Time your answers. Before the exam begins, write down the time it started, then add the time allowed for the examination and write down the time it must be completed, then divide the time available somewhat as follows:
    - If 3-1/2 hours are allowed, that would be 210 minutes. If you have 80 objective-type questions, that would be an average of 2-1/2 minutes per question. Allow yourself no more than 2 minutes per question, or a total of 160 minutes, which will permit about 50 minutes to review.
    - If for the time allotment of 210 minutes there are 7 essay questions to answer, that would average about 30 minutes a question. Give yourself only 25 minutes per question so that you have about 35 minutes to review.

6) The most important instruction is to *read each question* and make sure you know what is wanted. The second most important instruction is to *time yourself properly* so that you answer every question. The third most important instruction is to *answer every question*. Guess if you have to but include something for each question. Remember that you will receive no credit for a blank and will probably receive some credit if you write something in answer to an essay question. If you guess a letter – say "B" for a multiple-choice question – you may have guessed right. If you leave a blank as an answer to a multiple-choice question, the examiners may respect your feelings but it will not add a point to your score. Some exams may penalize you for wrong answers, so in such cases *only*, you may not want to guess unless you have some basis for your answer.

7) Suggestions
    a. Objective-type questions
        1. Examine the question booklet for proper sequence of pages and questions
        2. Read all instructions carefully
        3. Skip any question which seems too difficult; return to it after all other questions have been answered
        4. Apportion your time properly; do not spend too much time on any single question or group of questions

5. Note and underline key words – *all, most, fewest, least, best, worst, same, opposite*, etc.
6. Pay particular attention to negatives
7. Note unusual option, e.g., unduly long, short, complex, different or similar in content to the body of the question
8. Observe the use of "hedging" words – *probably, may, most likely*, etc.
9. Make sure that your answer is put next to the same number as the question
10. Do not second-guess unless you have good reason to believe the second answer is definitely more correct
11. Cross out original answer if you decide another answer is more accurate; do not erase until you are ready to hand your paper in
12. Answer all questions; guess unless instructed otherwise
13. Leave time for review

    b. Essay questions
1. Read each question carefully
2. Determine exactly what is wanted. Underline key words or phrases.
3. Decide on outline or paragraph answer
4. Include many different points and elements unless asked to develop any one or two points or elements
5. Show impartiality by giving pros and cons unless directed to select one side only
6. Make and write down any assumptions you find necessary to answer the questions
7. Watch your English, grammar, punctuation and choice of words
8. Time your answers; don't crowd material

8) Answering the essay question

Most essay questions can be answered by framing the specific response around several key words or ideas. Here are a few such key words or ideas:

M's: manpower, materials, methods, money, management
P's: purpose, program, policy, plan, procedure, practice, problems, pitfalls, personnel, public relations

    a. Six basic steps in handling problems:
1. Preliminary plan and background development
2. Collect information, data and facts
3. Analyze and interpret information, data and facts
4. Analyze and develop solutions as well as make recommendations
5. Prepare report and sell recommendations
6. Install recommendations and follow up effectiveness

    b. Pitfalls to avoid
1. *Taking things for granted* – A statement of the situation does not necessarily imply that each of the elements is necessarily true; for example, a complaint may be invalid and biased so that all that can be taken for granted is that a complaint has been registered

2. *Considering only one side of a situation* – Wherever possible, indicate several alternatives and then point out the reasons you selected the best one
3. *Failing to indicate follow up* – Whenever your answer indicates action on your part, make certain that you will take proper follow-up action to see how successful your recommendations, procedures or actions turn out to be
4. *Taking too long in answering any single question* – Remember to time your answers properly

IX. AFTER THE TEST

Scoring procedures differ in detail among civil service jurisdictions although the general principles are the same. Whether the papers are hand-scored or graded by machine we have described, they are nearly always graded by number. That is, the person who marks the paper knows only the number – never the name – of the applicant. Not until all the papers have been graded will they be matched with names. If other tests, such as training and experience or oral interview ratings have been given, scores will be combined. Different parts of the examination usually have different weights. For example, the written test might count 60 percent of the final grade, and a rating of training and experience 40 percent. In many jurisdictions, veterans will have a certain number of points added to their grades.

After the final grade has been determined, the names are placed in grade order and an eligible list is established. There are various methods for resolving ties between those who get the same final grade – probably the most common is to place first the name of the person whose application was received first. Job offers are made from the eligible list in the order the names appear on it. You will be notified of your grade and your rank as soon as all these computations have been made. This will be done as rapidly as possible.

People who are found to meet the requirements in the announcement are called "eligibles." Their names are put on a list of eligible candidates. An eligible's chances of getting a job depend on how high he stands on this list and how fast agencies are filling jobs from the list.

When a job is to be filled from a list of eligibles, the agency asks for the names of people on the list of eligibles for that job. When the civil service commission receives this request, it sends to the agency the names of the three people highest on this list. Or, if the job to be filled has specialized requirements, the office sends the agency the names of the top three persons who meet these requirements from the general list.

The appointing officer makes a choice from among the three people whose names were sent to him. If the selected person accepts the appointment, the names of the others are put back on the list to be considered for future openings.

That is the rule in hiring from all kinds of eligible lists, whether they are for typist, carpenter, chemist, or something else. For every vacancy, the appointing officer has his choice of any one of the top three eligibles on the list. This explains why the person whose name is on top of the list sometimes does not get an appointment when some of the persons lower on the list do. If the appointing officer chooses the second or third eligible, the No. 1 eligible does not get a job at once, but stays on the list until he is appointed or the list is terminated.

X. HOW TO PASS THE INTERVIEW TEST

The examination for which you applied requires an oral interview test. You have already taken the written test and you are now being called for the interview test – the final part of the formal examination.

You may think that it is not possible to prepare for an interview test and that there are no procedures to follow during an interview. Our purpose is to point out some things you can do in advance that will help you and some good rules to follow and pitfalls to avoid while you are being interviewed.

What is an interview supposed to test?

The written examination is designed to test the technical knowledge and competence of the candidate; the oral is designed to evaluate intangible qualities, not readily measured otherwise, and to establish a list showing the relative fitness of each candidate – as measured against his competitors – for the position sought. Scoring is not on the basis of "right" and "wrong," but on a sliding scale of values ranging from "not passable" to "outstanding." As a matter of fact, it is possible to achieve a relatively low score without a single "incorrect" answer because of evident weakness in the qualities being measured.

Occasionally, an examination may consist entirely of an oral test – either an individual or a group oral. In such cases, information is sought concerning the technical knowledges and abilities of the candidate, since there has been no written examination for this purpose. More commonly, however, an oral test is used to supplement a written examination.

Who conducts interviews?

The composition of oral boards varies among different jurisdictions. In nearly all, a representative of the personnel department serves as chairman. One of the members of the board may be a representative of the department in which the candidate would work. In some cases, "outside experts" are used, and, frequently, a businessman or some other representative of the general public is asked to serve. Labor and management or other special groups may be represented. The aim is to secure the services of experts in the appropriate field.

However the board is composed, it is a good idea (and not at all improper or unethical) to ascertain in advance of the interview who the members are and what groups they represent. When you are introduced to them, you will have some idea of their backgrounds and interests, and at least you will not stutter and stammer over their names.

What should be done before the interview?

While knowledge about the board members is useful and takes some of the surprise element out of the interview, there is other preparation which is more substantive. It *is* possible to prepare for an oral interview – in several ways:

1) Keep a copy of your application and review it carefully before the interview

This may be the only document before the oral board, and the starting point of the interview. Know what education and experience you have listed there, and the sequence and dates of all of it. Sometimes the board will ask you to review the highlights of your experience for them; you should not have to hem and haw doing it.

2) Study the class specification and the examination announcement

Usually, the oral board has one or both of these to guide them. The qualities, characteristics or knowledges required by the position sought are stated in these documents. They offer valuable clues as to the nature of the oral interview. For example, if the job involves supervisory responsibilities, the announcement will usually indicate that knowledge of modern supervisory methods and the qualifications of the candidate as a supervisor will be tested. If so, you can expect such questions, frequently in the form of a hypothetical situation which you are expected to solve. NEVER go into an oral without knowledge of the duties and responsibilities of the job you seek.

3) Think through each qualification required

Try to visualize the kind of questions you would ask if you were a board member. How well could you answer them? Try especially to appraise your own knowledge and background in each area, *measured against the job sought*, and identify any areas in which you are weak. Be critical and realistic – do not flatter yourself.

4) Do some general reading in areas in which you feel you may be weak

For example, if the job involves supervision and your past experience has NOT, some general reading in supervisory methods and practices, particularly in the field of human relations, might be useful. Do NOT study agency procedures or detailed manuals. The oral board will be testing your understanding and capacity, not your memory.

5) Get a good night's sleep and watch your general health and mental attitude

You will want a clear head at the interview. Take care of a cold or any other minor ailment, and of course, no hangovers.

What should be done on the day of the interview?

Now comes the day of the interview itself. Give yourself plenty of time to get there. Plan to arrive somewhat ahead of the scheduled time, particularly if your appointment is in the fore part of the day. If a previous candidate fails to appear, the board might be ready for you a bit early. By early afternoon an oral board is almost invariably behind schedule if there are many candidates, and you may have to wait. Take along a book or magazine to read, or your application to review, but leave any extraneous material in the waiting room when you go in for your interview. In any event, relax and compose yourself.

The matter of dress is important. The board is forming impressions about you – from your experience, your manners, your attitude, and your appearance. Give your personal appearance careful attention. Dress your best, but not your flashiest. Choose conservative, appropriate clothing, and be sure it is immaculate. This is a business interview, and your appearance should indicate that you regard it as such. Besides, being well groomed and properly dressed will help boost your confidence.

Sooner or later, someone will call your name and escort you into the interview room. *This is it.* From here on you are on your own. It is too late for any more preparation. But remember, you asked for this opportunity to prove your fitness, and you are here because your request was granted.

What happens when you go in?

The usual sequence of events will be as follows: The clerk (who is often the board stenographer) will introduce you to the chairman of the oral board, who will introduce you to the other members of the board. Acknowledge the introductions before you sit down. Do not be surprised if you find a microphone facing you or a stenotypist sitting by. Oral interviews are usually recorded in the event of an appeal or other review.

Usually the chairman of the board will open the interview by reviewing the highlights of your education and work experience from your application – primarily for the benefit of the other members of the board, as well as to get the material into the record. Do not interrupt or comment unless there is an error or significant misinterpretation; if that is the case, do not hesitate. But do not quibble about insignificant matters. Also, he will usually ask you some question about your education, experience or your present job – partly to get you to start talking and to establish the interviewing "rapport." He may start the actual questioning, or turn it over to one of the other members. Frequently, each member undertakes the questioning on a particular area, one in which he is perhaps most competent, so you can expect each member to participate in the examination. Because time is limited, you may also expect some rather abrupt switches in the direction the questioning takes, so do not be upset by it. Normally, a board member will not pursue a single line of questioning unless he discovers a particular strength or weakness.

After each member has participated, the chairman will usually ask whether any member has any further questions, then will ask you if you have anything you wish to add. Unless you are expecting this question, it may floor you. Worse, it may start you off on an extended, extemporaneous speech. The board is not usually seeking more information. The question is principally to offer you a last opportunity to present further qualifications or to indicate that you have nothing to add. So, if you feel that a significant qualification or characteristic has been overlooked, it is proper to point it out in a sentence or so. Do not compliment the board on the thoroughness of their examination – they have been sketchy, and you know it. If you wish, merely say, "No thank you, I have nothing further to add." This is a point where you can "talk yourself out" of a good impression or fail to present an important bit of information. Remember, *you close the interview yourself.*

The chairman will then say, "That is all, Mr. _____, thank you." Do not be startled; the interview is over, and quicker than you think. Thank him, gather your belongings and take your leave. Save your sigh of relief for the other side of the door.

How to put your best foot forward

Throughout this entire process, you may feel that the board individually and collectively is trying to pierce your defenses, seek out your hidden weaknesses and embarrass and confuse you. Actually, this is not true. They are obliged to make an appraisal of your qualifications for the job you are seeking, and they want to see you in your best light. Remember, they must interview all candidates and a non-cooperative candidate may become a failure in spite of their best efforts to bring out his qualifications. Here are 15 suggestions that will help you:

1) Be natural – Keep your attitude confident, not cocky

If you are not confident that you can do the job, do not expect the board to be. Do not apologize for your weaknesses, try to bring out your strong points. The board is interested in a positive, not negative, presentation. Cockiness will antagonize any board member and make him wonder if you are covering up a weakness by a false show of strength.

2) Get comfortable, but don't lounge or sprawl

Sit erectly but not stiffly. A careless posture may lead the board to conclude that you are careless in other things, or at least that you are not impressed by the importance of the occasion. Either conclusion is natural, even if incorrect. Do not fuss with your clothing, a pencil or an ashtray. Your hands may occasionally be useful to emphasize a point; do not let them become a point of distraction.

3) Do not wisecrack or make small talk

This is a serious situation, and your attitude should show that you consider it as such. Further, the time of the board is limited – they do not want to waste it, and neither should you.

4) Do not exaggerate your experience or abilities

In the first place, from information in the application or other interviews and sources, the board may know more about you than you think. Secondly, you probably will not get away with it. An experienced board is rather adept at spotting such a situation, so do not take the chance.

5) If you know a board member, do not make a point of it, yet do not hide it

Certainly you are not fooling him, and probably not the other members of the board. Do not try to take advantage of your acquaintanceship – it will probably do you little good.

6) Do not dominate the interview

Let the board do that. They will give you the clues – do not assume that you have to do all the talking. Realize that the board has a number of questions to ask you, and do not try to take up all the interview time by showing off your extensive knowledge of the answer to the first one.

7) Be attentive

You only have 20 minutes or so, and you should keep your attention at its sharpest throughout. When a member is addressing a problem or question to you, give him your undivided attention. Address your reply principally to him, but do not exclude the other board members.

8) Do not interrupt

A board member may be stating a problem for you to analyze. He will ask you a question when the time comes. Let him state the problem, and wait for the question.

9) Make sure you understand the question

Do not try to answer until you are sure what the question is. If it is not clear, restate it in your own words or ask the board member to clarify it for you. However, do not haggle about minor elements.

10) Reply promptly but not hastily

A common entry on oral board rating sheets is "candidate responded readily," or "candidate hesitated in replies." Respond as promptly and quickly as you can, but do not jump to a hasty, ill-considered answer.

11) Do not be peremptory in your answers

A brief answer is proper – but do not fire your answer back. That is a losing game from your point of view. The board member can probably ask questions much faster than you can answer them.

12) Do not try to create the answer you think the board member wants

He is interested in what kind of mind you have and how it works – not in playing games. Furthermore, he can usually spot this practice and will actually grade you down on it.

13) Do not switch sides in your reply merely to agree with a board member

Frequently, a member will take a contrary position merely to draw you out and to see if you are willing and able to defend your point of view. Do not start a debate, yet do not surrender a good position. If a position is worth taking, it is worth defending.

14) Do not be afraid to admit an error in judgment if you are shown to be wrong

The board knows that you are forced to reply without any opportunity for careful consideration. Your answer may be demonstrably wrong. If so, admit it and get on with the interview.

15) Do not dwell at length on your present job

The opening question may relate to your present assignment. Answer the question but do not go into an extended discussion. You are being examined for a *new* job, not your present one. As a matter of fact, try to phrase ALL your answers in terms of the job for which you are being examined.

Basis of Rating

Probably you will forget most of these "do's" and "don'ts" when you walk into the oral interview room. Even remembering them all will not ensure you a passing grade. Perhaps you did not have the qualifications in the first place. But remembering them will help you to put your best foot forward, without treading on the toes of the board members.

Rumor and popular opinion to the contrary notwithstanding, an oral board wants you to make the best appearance possible. They know you are under pressure – but they also want to see how you respond to it as a guide to what your reaction would be under the pressures of the job you seek. They will be influenced by the degree of poise you display, the personal traits you show and the manner in which you respond.

ABOUT THIS BOOK

This book contains tests divided into Examination Sections. Go through each test, answering every question in the margin. We have also attached a sample answer sheet at the back of the book that can be removed and used. At the end of each test look at the answer key and check your answers. On the ones you got wrong, look at the right answer choice and learn. Do not fill in the answers first. Do not memorize the questions and answers, but understand the answer and principles involved. On your test, the questions will likely be different from the samples. Questions are changed and new ones added. If you understand these past questions you should have success with any changes that arise. Tests may consist of several types of questions. We have additional books on each subject should more study be advisable or necessary for you. Finally, the more you study, the better prepared you will be. This book is intended to be the last thing you study before you walk into the examination room. Prior study of relevant texts is also recommended. NLC publishes some of these in our Fundamental Series. Knowledge and good sense are important factors in passing your exam. Good luck also helps. So now study this Passbook, absorb the material contained within and take that knowledge into the examination. Then do your best to pass that exam.

EXAMINATION SECTION

EXAMINATION SECTION
TEST 1

DIRECTIONS: Each question or incomplete statement is followed by several suggested answers or completions. Select the one that BEST answers the question or completes the statement. *PRINT THE LETTER OF THE CORRECT ANSWER IN THE SPACE AT THE RIGHT.*

1. When you are first appointed as a trackman, your superior will PROBABLY expect you to   1._____

    A. make many costly mistakes
    B. pay close attention to instructions
    C. do very little work
    D. make many suggestions

2. Helmets are frequently worn by workers for protection against   2._____

    A. moving machinery
    B. fire
    C. electric shock
    D. falling objects

3. In order to prevent hand injuries, it would be a good idea for a trackman to wear work gloves when   3._____

    A. walking next to the tracks
    B. handling large tools
    C. cutting cord
    D. sorting small screws

4. A trackman should know that if a bag of cement got wet, the cement would   4._____

    A. crumble
    B. harden
    C. wash away
    D. evaporate

5. Of several pieces of pipe of equal size and length, the LIGHTEST would be made of   5._____

    A. cast iron
    B. wrought iron
    C. aluminum
    D. brass

6. Newly appointed trackmen are instructed in the use of fire extinguishers MAINLY   6._____

    A. to be able to use one when necessary
    B. because they are not able to do the more important work
    C. because they may be the cause of fires due to their inexperience
    D. to interest them in fire prevention

7. Safety on any job is BEST assured by   7._____

    A. working very slowly
    B. following every rule
    C. never working alone
    D. keeping alert

8. The piston of a hydraulic jack is caused to move by   8._____

    A. air pressure
    B. electricity
    C. oil pressure
    D. steam pressure

1

9. If a metal bar cracks when struck a blow by a hammer, the metal is MOST likely to be

   A. copper
   B. cast iron
   C. lead
   D. steel

10. Trackmen are required to report defective equipment to their supervisors, even when the maintenance of the defective equipment is handled entirely by another department.
    The purpose of this requirement is evidently to

    A. prevent accidents
    B. fix responsibility
    C. discourage slackers
    D. encourage alertness

11. The proper tool to use when tightening a large nut on a bolt is the

    A. screwdriver
    B. gas plier
    C. open-end wrench
    D. brace and bit

12. To make a 1-inch diameter hole in a concrete wall, it is proper to use a

    A. star drill and hammer
    B. reamer and hammer
    C. lag screw
    D. countersink

13. The tool that MUST be sharpened on an oilstone is a

    A. ripsaw
    B. center punch
    C. twist drill
    D. carpenter's chisel

14. The BEST tool to use to open a wooden packing case is a

    A. carpenter's chisel
    B. flat wrench
    C. crate opener
    D. carpenter's saw

15. When a job on the subway tracks is finished, all tools that were used should be picked up and removed from the place where the work was done.
    The MOST important reason for following this procedure is that tools left behind may

    A. rust
    B. get lost
    C. be needed somewhere else
    D. cause an accident

Questions 16-23.

DIRECTIONS: Questions 16 through 23, inclusive, are based on the article about general safety precautions given below. Refer to this article in answering these questions.

GENERAL SAFETY PRECAUTIONS

When work is being done on or next to a track on which regular trains are running, special signals must be displayed as called for in the general rules for flagging. Yellow caution signals, green clear signals, and a flagman with a red danger signal are required for the protection of traffic and the workmen in accordance with the standard flagging rules. The flagman shall also carry a white signal for display to the motorman when he may proceed. The foreman in charge must see that proper signals are displayed.

On elevated lines during daylight hours, the yellow signal shall be a yellow flag, the red signal shall be a red flag, the green signal shall be a green flag, and the white signal shall be a white flag. In subway sections, and on elevated lines after dark, the yellow signal shall be a yellow lantern, the red signal shall be a red lantern, the green signal shall be a green lantern, and the white signal shall be a white lantern.

Caution and clear signals are to be secured to the elevated or subway structure with non-metallic fastenings outside the clearance line of the train and on the motorman's side of the track.

16. On elevated lines during daylight hours, the caution signal is a

    A. yellow lantern
    B. green lantern
    C. yellow flag
    D. green flag

17. In subway sections, the clear signal is a

    A. yellow lantern
    B. green lantern
    C. yellow flag
    D. green flag

18. The number of lanterns in the hands of the flagman in a subway section is

    A. 1
    B. 2
    C. 3
    D. 4

19. A suitable fastening for securing caution or clear signals to the structure is

    A. a steel C-clamp
    B. brass binding wire
    C. heavy twine
    D. picture wire

20. On an elevated line, the red flag is evidently

    A. held by the flagman
    B. secured to the structure
    C. carried by the motorman
    D. displayed by the workmen

21. The signal displayed by the flagman for a motorman in the subway to proceed is a

    A. green lantern
    B. yellow flag
    C. red flag
    D. white lantern

22. The caution, clear, and danger signals are displayed for the information of

    A. flagmen
    B. workmen
    C. motormen
    D. foremen

23. Since the motorman's operating position is on the right-hand side of the train, the caution and clear signals should be secured to the

    A. structure to the right of the track
    B. right-hand running rail
    C. left-hand running rail
    D. structure to the left of the track

Questions 24-31.

DIRECTIONS: Questions 24 through 31 are based on the sketch below showing one of the track rails on a section of track (as you would see it if you were standing on the track looking down). The track rail rests directly on a tie plate at each tie and is fastened to each tie by spikes. The rail braces are placed over the tie plates.

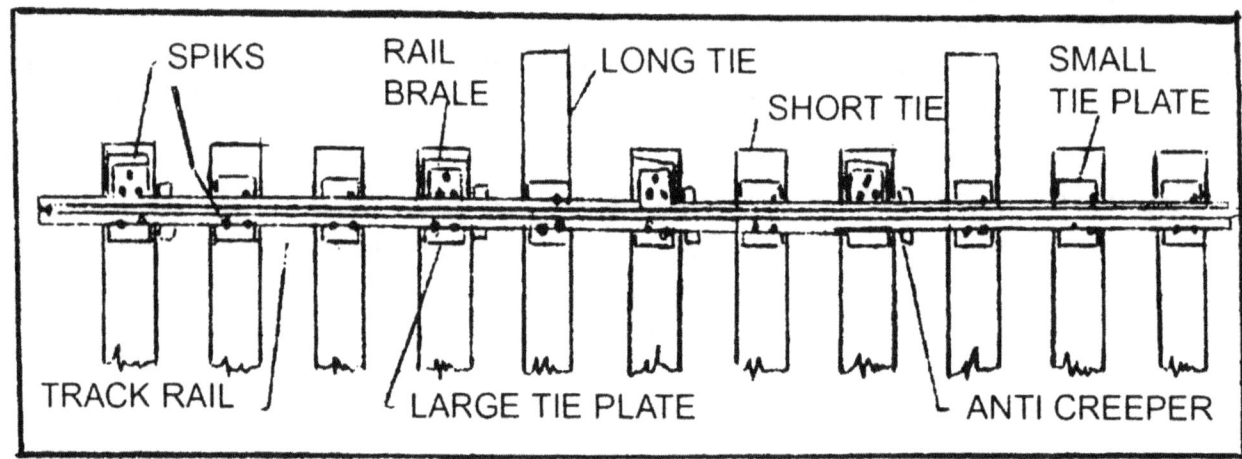

24. The total number of short ties shown is

    A. 2 B. 4 C. 5 D. 9

25. The number of short ties shown with large tie plates is

    A. 2 B. 4 C. 5 D. 9

26. The number of short ties shown with small tie plates is

    A. 2 B. 4 C. 5 D. 9

27. The number of spikes shown on each long tie is

    A. 2 B. 3 C. 4 D. 5

28. The number of anti-creepers shown is

    A. 1 B. 2 C. 3 D. 4

29. When installing the spikes, it is reasonable to expect that the installer would use some kind of

    A. hammer B. screwdriver
    C. punch   D. gimlet

30. The sketch shows that rail braces are installed on _____ ties.

    A. all short B. all long
    C. some short D. some long

31. It is reasonable to expect a candidate for trackman to know that the ties are

    A. concrete B. soft iron
    C. hard rubber D. wood

Questions 32-39.

DIRECTIONS: Questions 32 through 39 are based on the paragraph about stone ballast given below. Refer to this paragraph in answering these questions.

STONE BALLAST

Stone ballast for the tracks consists of pieces of trap rock or limestone which do not show any signs of cracking or breaking apart. Rubble, slate, and shale are not used. The largest pieces of ballast are those that will just pass through a hole 1 1/4" square, and the smallest pieces are those that will not pass through a hole 1/2" square. Ballast properly placed and tamped prevents movement of the cross ties from side to side and also keeps the ties from moving in either direction along the rails. Ballast also helps to spread the weight of trains evenly over the roadbed and allows water to drain away quickly from the cross ties and rails. When stone ballast becomes so filled with dirt and other substances so that drainage is interfered with, it is cleaned or replaced.

32. Ballast may consist of

    A. slate   B. limestone   C. shale   D. rubble

33. The largest piece of ballast will NOT pass through a square hole measuring, on each side,

    A. 1 3/4"   B. 1 1/2"   C. 1 1/4"   D. 1"

34. The shape of MOST pieces of ballast is evidently

    A. square   B. round   C. oblong   D. irregular

35. Ballast helps to

    A. waterproof the track
    B. keep the rails spread apart
    C. spread train weight evenly
    D. hold the track down on the roadbed

36. Ballast is cleaned or replaced when it

    A. will not pass through a 1/2" square hole
    B. shows signs of breaking apart
    C. becomes filled with dirt
    D. becomes too tightly tamped

37. Ballast prevents

    A. movement of the cross ties
    B. dirt from collecting on the tracks
    C. crushing of the cross ties
    D. cracking of the roadbed

38. Ballast provides drainage because

    A. it supports the cross ties
    B. there are spaces between the stones
    C. there are spaces between the cross ties
    D. it is tamped firmly

39. By logical reasoning, the number of screens necessary to select the proper sizes of stones for ballast is

   A. 1   B. 2   C. 3   D. 4

40. To check, without actually measuring, that the distance between the two rails of a track is the standard distance, it would be logical to use a

   A. rail gauge
   B. knotted string
   C. yardstick
   D. ten-foot pole

Questions 41-49.

DIRECTIONS: Questions 41 through 49 are based on knowledge of the subway that can be acquired by an observant, interested person. Think of what you have noticed about the subway in answering these questions.

41. Spikes used to hold the running rails in place are MOST NEARLY like

   A. ice picks
   B. large nails
   C. shelf brackets
   D. C-clamps

42. The third rail is

   A. one of the running rails
   B. located between the running rails
   C. suspended from the subway roof
   D. placed to one side of the running rails

43. The color of the top surface of the running rails that are in regular use is

   A. reddish-brown
   B. light blue
   C. silver-grey
   D. deep yellow

44. The height of a station platform above the running rails is CLOSEST to

   A. 6"   B. 1'   C. 4'   D. 10'

45. Of the four lights at the front of a train, the color of the two lower ones is always

   A. red   B. white   C. blue   D. green

46. The color of the four lights at the rear of every train is

   A. red   B. white   C. blue   D. green

47. The running rails do NOT

   A. support train weight
   B. guide train wheels
   C. provide smooth riding surfaces for the wheels
   D. rest directly on the concrete roadbed

48. The regular clicking sound heard as a train rolls along is due to the

    A. irregularities in the train wheels
    B. wheels striking the joints in the rails
    C. switching on and off of the driving motors
    D. rattling of the car windows

49. The number of wheels on each car of MOST subway trains is

    A. 4   B. 6   C. 8   D. 12

50. A steel rail will increase in length if the

    A. humidity decreases
    C. humidity increases
    B. temperature decreases
    D. temperature increases

KEY (CORRECT ANSWERS)

1. B	11. C	21. D	31. D	41. B
2. D	12. A	22. C	32. B	42. D
3. B	13. D	23. A	33. D	43. C
4. B	14. C	24. D	34. D	44. C
5. C	15. D	25. B	35. C	45. B
6. A	16. C	26. C	36. C	46. A
7. D	17. B	27. B	37. A	47. D
8. C	18. B	28. D	38. B	48. B
9. B	19. C	29. A	39. B	49. C
10. A	20. A	30. C	40. A	50. D

TEST 2

DIRECTIONS: Each question or incomplete statement is followed by several suggested answers or completions. Select the one that BEST answers the question or completes the statement. *PRINT THE LETTER OF THE CORRECT ANSWER IN THE SPACE AT THE RIGHT.*

1. Railroad ties are creosoted MAINLY to make them

    A. black
    B. last longer
    C. look better
    D. slippery

2. Trackmen are cautioned, as a safety measure, not to use water to extinguish fires near the 600-volt third rail. The MOST important reason for this caution is that the water

    A. may transmit electrical shock to the user
    B. will cause harmful steam
    C. will cause the running rails to become slippery
    D. may damage the equipment

3. It is logical to expect that a trackman in the subway MUST

    A. test to see if the third rail is alive as he goes along
    B. carry a timetable
    C. carry a lighted lantern
    D. walk on a running rail at local stations

4. A length of running rail in common use weighs 1300 pounds. If such a length of rail is picked up using 6 tongs with two men on each tong, the weight lifted per man is about _____ lbs.

    A. 110   B. 130   C. 215   D. 260

5. By logical reasoning, you would expect to find the heaviest accumulation of oil that has dripped from train bearings onto the trackway

    A. near track switches
    B. in subway stations
    C. halfway between stations
    D. in the middle of curves

6. The MOST important reason for wearing goggles when working on subway track is to

    A. shield the eyes from glare
    B. improve vision
    C. reduce eye strain
    D. avoid eye injuries

7. The proper tool to use to cut off a length of rail is the

    A. hacksaw
    B. cold chisel
    C. metal cutting shear
    D. ax

8. The transit authority does not want trackmen to wear loose-fitting clothing when working, MAINLY because such clothing

    A. might interfere when the trackmen are using heavy tools
    B. encourages carelessness
    C. makes a poor impression on the public
    D. might catch onto a part of a passing train

9. The replacement of track rails in the subway is done at night MAINLY because

   A. the tunnels are dark both day and night
   B. trains make better time at night
   C. many men prefer night work
   D. fewer trains run at night

10. It is reasonable to expect that a trackman would NOT ordinarily be required to

    A. make minor repairs to the track
    B. carry heavy tools
    C. detain disorderly people
    D. know how to use the telephone

11. If a trackman notices a pile of oily rags while he is working in the subway, he should report it to his superior, MAINLY because the rags

    A. may catch fire
    B. may be a nest for rats
    C. make the area look dirty
    D. might cause another trackman to trip

Questions 12-19.

DIRECTIONS: Questions 12 through 19 are based on the information contained in the rules for reporting fires given below. Read the rules carefully before answering these questions.

RULES FOR REPORTING FIRES

If a fire occurs in the subway or in the cars, the person discovering same shall, except in the case of very small fires, go to the nearest telephone and notify the trainmaster. If a fire occurs on a bus, the person discovering same shall, except in the case of very small fires, go to the nearest telephone and notify the Central Dispatch Office. In both cases, the person making the call should give the location of the fire, his name, his badge number, and the department in which employed. In the case of a very small fire, the person discovering same shall use all means in his power to extinguish it promptly using fire extinguishers, sand pails, water buckets, or other equipment readily available. A complete report of the fire, including the location from which the extinguisher or other equipment was taken, should be transmitted promptly to the employee's department head.

12. A fire discovered in the subway should be reported to the

    A. fire department   B. police department
    C. trainmaster   D. Central Dispatch Office

13. A fire discovered on a bus should be reported to the

    A. fire department   B. police department
    C. trainmaster   D. Central Dispatch Office

14. The employee discovering a fire should report same by use of the NEAREST

    A. fire alarm box   B. gong
    C. telephone   D. messenger

15. A trackman on duty is LEAST likely to discover a fire

    A. in the subway   B. on an elevated line
    C. on a bus   D. in a train storage yard

16. The employee discovering a very small fire should

    A. notify the trainmaster immediately
    B. wait and see if it will spread before reporting it
    C. go for assistance to extinguish it
    D. try to put it out promptly

17. An employee's report on a very small fire would NOT include the

    A. cost to repair the damage
    B. name of the employee reporting
    C. location of the extinguisher used
    D. date on which the fire occurred

18. The employee's complete report of a fire must identify the extinguisher used MAINLY so that

    A. it will be refilled or replaced
    B. its effectiveness can be checked
    C. the location of the fire will be recorded
    D. its contents will not be wasted

19. For large fires, the complete report required in the last sentence of the above rules is a written report because

    A. a written report is most accurate
    B. the fire may involve a criminal offense
    C. the original report was made orally
    D. it provides a permanent record

Questions 20-26.

DIRECTIONS: Questions 20 through 26 are based on the following sketch showing a brick wall. Refer to this sketch when answering these questions.

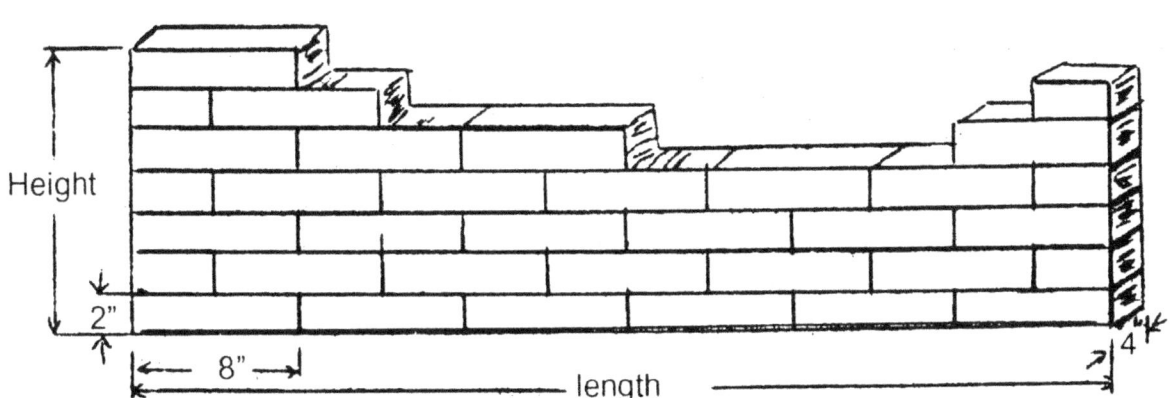

20. The number of whole bricks in the LOWEST layer is

    A. 4   B. 5   C. 6   D. 7

21. The total number of half-bricks shown is

    A. 3   B. 4   C. 5   D. 6

22. The height of the left end of the wall is

    A. 12"   B. 14"   C. 24"   D. 48"

23. The length of the wall is

    A. 2'   B. 3'   C. 4'   D. 5'

24. The number of whole bricks required to just complete the sixth layer across the entire length of the wall is

    A. 7   B. 6   C. 5   D. 4

25. The total number of whole bricks required to complete the wall to the uniform height of the seventh layer is

    A. 11   B. 9   C. 8   D. 7

26. To complete a wall that is 4" lower than the *height* indicated, you would have to add 2 whole bricks and remove

    A. 1 whole brick and 3 half-bricks
    B. 2 whole bricks and 2 half-bricks
    C. 3 whole bricks and 1 half-brick
    D. 4 whole bricks

27. As a rule, gasoline for use in trackmen's headquarters is stored in special closed containers.
    The MOST important reason for the use of closed containers is to

    A. prevent theft   B. reduce fire hazard
    C. confine the odor   D. prevent contamination

28. Each employee using supplies from one of the first aid kits available throughout the subway is required to submit a report of the occurrence.
The MOST likely reason for requiring said report is so that the

   A. employee may be given credit for his action
   B. used material will be sure to be replaced
   C. employee may be charged for the material
   D. doctor can check if the proper first aid was given

29. When official forms are to be filled out by employees, it is sometimes requested that certain information be printed rather than written.
This is MAINLY because printing

   A. is easier to do
   B. can be done in pencil
   C. is easier to read
   D. takes less space

30. The CHIEF purpose of administering artificial respiration in first aid is to

   A. exert regular pressure on the heart
   B. force the blood into circulation by pressure
   C. force air into the lungs
   D. keep the person warm by keeping his body in motion

31. When severe shock occurs, it is IMPORTANT for the person being treated to have

   A. sedatives and cold drinks
   B. warmth and low head position
   C. hot drinks and much activity
   D. sedatives and sitting position

32. When administering first aid, a tourniquet is used to

   A. sterilize the injured area
   B. hold the splints in place
   C. hold the dressing in place
   D. stop the loss of blood

33. Every employee is required by the rules to give advance notice of his intention to be absent from work.
The LOGICAL reason for having such a requirement is to

   A. check if the employee has a good excuse
   B. provide a substitute if necessary
   C. change the payroll records
   D. find out about the employee's next assignment

34. The MAXIMUM number of 2" by 3" rectangular pieces which can be cut from a 5" by 6" rectangular piece is

   A. 3   B. 4   C. 5   D. 6

35. The MOST important reason for roping off a work area on a subway station is to prevent

   A. distraction of the crew by the public
   B. injuries to the repair crew
   C. injury to the public
   D. delays to the public

36. The designation two-by-four is FREQUENTLY used to describe a   36.____

   A. piece of lumber   B. bolt
   C. carpenter's square   D. steel beam

37. To make a leak-resistant joint between two pieces of metal, it is LEAST desirable to use   37.____

   A. caulking   B. solder   C. concrete   D. a gasket

38. A gauge number is used in connection with sheet metal to specify its   38.____

   A. length   B. width
   C. thickness   D. area

39. An employee MUST notify the office whenever he changes his address.   39.____
   The LOGICAL reason for this requirement is to

   A. enable the authority to furnish correct information to other city agencies
   B. enable the authority to contact the employee in time of need
   C. prevent the holding of two jobs
   D. help the post office, if requested

40. Employees must know the rules and regulations governing their jobs to   40.____

   A. please their supervisors
   B. foresee emergencies
   C. avoid accidents
   D. perform their duties properly

41. When a piece of old equipment is taken apart, the fastening devices that are MOST likely   41.____
    to be reusable are the

   A. bolts   B. nails
   C. cotter pins   D. rivets

42. When an ambulance is required because someone is injured in the subway, trackmen   42.____
    are instructed to telephone the transit police department and have the transit police call
    for the ambulance.
    It is MOST important for a trackman to tell the transit police

   A. how severe the injuries are
   B. his own name and badge number
   C. whether the injured party is male or female
   D. where the ambulance is needed

43. An important reason for having a trackman follow the procedure of Question 42 above,   43.____
    instead of personally calling for the ambulance, is to

   A. provide faster service
   B. avoid duplication of calls
   C. fix responsibility
   D. enable the trackman to concentrate on his work

44. A trackman on duty in the subway notices a stranger in ordinary street clothes walking along the track toward him. The trackman calls out to the stranger to find out who he is, whereupon the stranger turns around and runs away.
The BEST action on the part of the trackman is to

   A. run after the stranger
   B. forget about the incident
   C. report the occurrence promptly from the nearest telephone
   D. shout after the stranger and tell him to come back

45. If a trackman has a poor accident record, it would be LOGICAL to assume that this trackman probably is

   A. unlucky   B. careless
   C. over-cautious   D. safety-conscious

46. Artificial respiration should be started immediately on a trackman who has suffered an electric shock by coming in contact with the third rail if he is

   A. conscious but badly burned
   B. unconscious and breathing heavily
   C. conscious but in a daze
   D. unconscious and not breathing

47. When administering first aid for the accidental swallowing of poison, water is given CHIEFLY to

   A. increase energy   B. quiet the nerves
   C. weaken the poison   D. prevent choking

48. The recommended first aid procedure for a person who has fainted is to lay him down with his head lower than his body.
Such a position is used because it

   A. quickly relieves exhaustion
   B. speeds the return of blood to the head
   C. retards rapid breathing
   D. is the most comfortable position

49. To change from Daylight Saving Time to Standard Time, the hands of the clock are moved _____ in _____.

   A. ahead; spring   B. ahead; autumn
   C. back; spring   D. back; autumn

50. If you are assigned by your foreman to a job which you do not understand, you should

   A. explain this to the foreman and request further instructions from him
   B. try to do the job anyway because you learn from experience
   C. ask another trackman to explain the job
   D. ask another foreman since your foreman should have explained the job when it was assigned

KEY (CORRECT ANSWERS)

1. B	11. A	21. D	31. D	41. A
2. A	12. C	22. B	32. D	42. D
3. C	13. D	23. C	33. B	43. B
4. A	14. C	24. D	34. C	44. C
5. B	15. C	25. A	35. C	45. B
6. D	16. D	26. B	36. A	46. D
7. A	17. A	27. B	37. C	47. C
8. D	18. A	28. B	38. C	48. B
9. D	19. D	29. C	39. B	49. D
10. C	20. C	30. C	40. D	50. A

TEST 3

DIRECTIONS: Each question or incomplete statement is followed by several suggested answers or completions. Select the one that BEST answers the question or completes the statement. *PRINT THE LETTER OF THE CORRECT ANSWER IN THE SPACE AT THE RIGHT.*

1. When track work is being done on the elevated structure, canvas spreads are suspended under the working area MAINLY to 1.___
   - A. reduce noise
   - B. discourage crowds
   - C. protect the structure
   - D. protect pedestrians

2. The MOST important reason for maintaining correct spacing between track ties is to 2.___
   - A. provide good track support
   - B. use fewer ties
   - C. make trackwalking safe
   - D. use fewer joints

3. The MAIN reason employees are forbidden to hang flags or lights of any description on subway signals is to avoid 3.___
   - A. fire hazard
   - B. damage to signal equipment
   - C. confusing the motormen
   - D. loss of such articles

4. The train schedules available at stations are provided MAINLY for the use of the 4.___
   - A. motormen
   - B. conductors
   - C. passengers
   - D. dispatchers

5. Spare replacement rails are provided along the subway track.
   This is done MAINLY to 5.___
   - A. reduce hauling costs
   - B. save repair time
   - C. age the rails
   - D. save storage space

6. Of the following, the MOST dangerous track condition for a train is a 6.___
   - A. shiny rail
   - B. slightly worn rail
   - C. wet tie
   - D. broken rail

7. A good fireproof material is 7.___
   - A. asbestos
   - B. canvas
   - C. wool
   - D. cotton

8. The wall area behind the metal ladders permanently fastened into the subway wall is often painted yellow in order to 8.___
   - A. prevent accumulation of dirt
   - B. make the ladders easily visible
   - C. prevent rusting of the fastenings
   - D. reduce reflection from the wall

9. A trackman's pick has a split handle near the head of the tool.
   The trackman should 9.___
   - A. tape the handle
   - B. shorten the handle by cutting off the split part
   - C. report it to his foreman
   - D. nail the split part together

10. Car wheels are MOST likely to squeal when trains are

    A. leaving stations
    B. coasting on straight track
    C. speeding on straight track
    D. running on curved track

11. Track rails being unloaded from a work train are generally lifted off or skidded to the ground, rather than dropped. This is done MAINLY to avoid

    A. damaging the rails
    B. damage to the work train
    C. noise
    D. jarring the signals

12. Tool boxes are used along the subway tracks for storing tools. This is to

    A. keep the tools safe
    B. keep the tools clean
    C. prevent excessive use of the tools
    D. prevent damage to the tools

13. Hands and feet should be kept away from track switches MAINLY because the switch

    A. is fragile
    B. is insulated
    C. may move suddenly
    D. is lubricated

14. The MAIN reason for constantly inspecting tracks is to

    A. keep the trackmen busy
    B. reduce the cost of track repairs
    C. improve train schedules
    D. remove safety hazards

15. Heavy accumulations of oil and grease on the tracks are generally found at stations. This is because

    A. more lubrication is required at these locations
    B. it makes for quicker train stops
    C. it makes for easier train starts
    D. of drippings from trains during station stops

16. Spaces large enough for a man to stand in are provided in the subway wall MAINLY for

    A. storing track rails
    B. the safety of employees
    C. drainage
    D. unloading of material

17. The MOST important information a trackman should have on his first day of work on the tracks is

    A. the name of his superintendent
    B. knowledge of safety rules
    C. data on train running speeds
    D. the names of his co-workers

18. It would NOT be advisable to re-use a

   A. cotter pin
   B. machine bolt
   C. lag screw
   D. wood screw

19. Before stepping on a subway track, a trackman should

   A. see if power is on
   B. turn his lantern off
   C. look up and down the track
   D. notify the foreman

20. As a newly appointed trackman, your foreman would expect you to

   A. do all the hard work
   B. study trackwork on your own time
   C. follow his instructions closely
   D. make many blunders

21. The metal which is MOST likely to crack when struck a heavy blow is

   A. malleable iron
   B. forged steel
   C. cast iron
   D. wrought iron

22. The MOST important reason for wearing strong heavy shoes when working on subway track is to

   A. avoid colds
   B. obtain longer wear
   C. reduce fatigue
   D. avoid injury

23. Many trackmen working close together at the same location is NOT an advisable procedure mainly because of

   A. waste of manpower
   B. possible injury from each other's tools
   C. the danger of approaching trains
   D. difficulty in supervising them

24. When trackmen are working on track in service, a whistle is used to indicate

   A. power is on
   B. power is off
   C. the approach of a train
   D. the signal system is to be disconnected

25. Pneumatic hammers are operated by

   A. compressed air
   B. acetylene
   C. water pressure
   D. oil pressure

26. If a trackman working on the tracks has a heart attack, the BEST immediate action to take is to

    A. walk him to the nearest station
    B. massage his hands
    C. carry him to a place of safety
    D. keep his head up

27. Holding a spike maul on the head of a spike and hitting the maul with another maul is prohibited because of the danger of

    A. flying metal
    B. bending the spike
    C. driving the spike too tightly
    D. fire hazard from flying sparks

28. A trackman walking track notices a man standing nearby on the trackway and believes from the man's actions that he nay have no business being there.
    The trackman should

    A. continue with his work and ignore the man
    B. immediately order the man off the roadway
    C. hold the man for questioning by the police
    D. determine if the man has proper authorization

29. The MOST important reason for removing pressure from an air hose before breaking the hose connection is to avoid

    A. fire hazard   B. personal injury
    C. waste   D. air compressor damage

30. Steel helmets give workers the MOST protection from

    A. electric shock   B. eye injuries
    C. fire   D. falling objects

Questions 31-39.

DIRECTIONS: Questions 31 through 39 are based on the information contained in the INSTRUCTIONS ON TRACKWORK given below. Read these rules carefully before answering these questions.

INSTRUCTIONS ON TRACKWORK

Tie plates shall be used under rails on all ties except at insulated joints. Bolts through insulating bushings are not to be driven through, but inserted by hand. Guard rails are to be bolted to running rails with standard bolts, using spring washers, head locks, and flat washers. Rail braces shall be spiked with screw spikes. When removing or reinserting screw spikes, care must be taken not to destroy the thread in the wood tie. If a cut spike (nail type) is withdrawn for any reason, the hole is to be filled with a square creosoted plug and the spike re-driven in the same location. Ties are to be pulled by hand. No picks, shovels or spike mauls are to be used for pulling ties.

31. Ties should be pulled

    A. with spike mauls
    B. with shovels
    C. by hand
    D. with picks

32. Tie plates are used

    A. on all ties
    B. only at insulated joints
    C. except at insulated joints
    D. on alternate ties

33. Rail braces shall have

    A. insulators
    B. bolts
    C. cut spikes
    D. screw spikes

34. Plugs are to be

    A. square
    B. free of creosote
    C. round
    D. driven by hand

35. Guard rails are fastened to running rails with

    A. special bolts
    B. standard bolts
    C. insulators
    D. plugs

36. Bolts through insulating bushings are to be

    A. hand inserted
    B. non-standard
    C. elliptical
    D. driven

37. When cut spikes are withdrawn from a tie, the hole is to be

    A. insulated
    B. rethreaded
    C. left open
    D. plugged

38. Head locks and spring washers are used on

    A. guard rail bolts
    B. screw spikes
    C. tie plates
    D. cut spikes

39. Screw spike holes in a tie

    A. may be reused
    B. must be plugged with a round plug
    C. are not to be reused
    D. must always be rethreaded

Questions 40-48.

DIRECTIONS: Questions 40 through 48 are based on the following sketch showing a pile of track ties, all of equal size. Refer to this sketch when answering these questions.

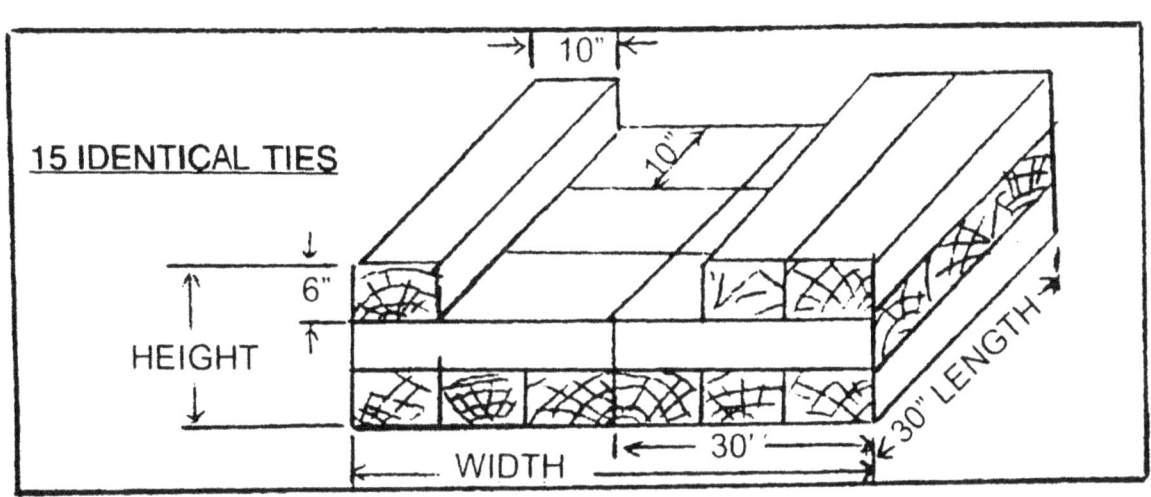

40. The size of each tie is

    A. 8" x 10" x 30"
    B. 6" x 8" x 30"
    C. 6" x 8" x 60"
    D. 6" x 10" x 30"

41. The width of the pile is

    A. 30"   B. 36"   C. 48"   D. 60"

42. The SMALLEST dimension of the pile is the

    A. height   B. length   C. width   D. perimeter

43. The length of the pile is equal to _____ the width.

    A. 1/4
    B. 1/2
    C. 3/4
    D. none of the above

44. To reduce the pile shown to a MAXIMUM height of 6", the number of ties to be removed is

    A. 3   B. 6   C. 9   D. 12

45. The pile shown can be filled solid to an even height of 18" by adding _____ ties.

    A. two   B. three   C. four   D. six

46. When the pile shown is filled solid to an even height of 18", the total number of ties in the pile will be

    A. 15   B. 18   C. 21   D. 24

47. The MAXIMUM number of blocks 6" x 10" x 4" which can be cut from one tie is

    A. 3   B. 5   C. 7   D. 8

48. If a number of the ties are to be laid lengthwise, end to end, to form a section 10' long, then the number of ties required is

    A. 2   B. 3   C. 4   D. 5

49. Because of the high voltage rail, it would be BEST for trackmen to use work pails made of 49.___

   A. iron B. steel C. fibre D. brass

50. Extreme care should be taken to use a file properly because it is 50.___

   A. very ductile
   B. very malleable
   C. extremely hard and rather brittle
   D. annealed and very soft

KEY (CORRECT ANSWERS)

1. D	11. A	21. C	31. C	41. D
2. A	12. A	22. D	32. C	42. A
3. C	13. C	23. B	33. D	43. B
4. C	14. D	24. C	34. A	44. C
5. B	15. D	25. A	35. B	45. B
6. D	16. B	26. C	36. A	46. B
7. A	17. B	27. A	37. D	47. C
8. B	18. A	28. D	38. A	48. C
9. C	19. C	29. B	39. A	49. C
10. D	20. C	30. D	40. D	50. C

TEST 4

DIRECTIONS: Each question or incomplete statement is followed by several suggested answers or completions. Select the one that BEST answers the question or completes the statement. *PRINT THE LETTER OF THE CORRECT ANSWER IN THE SPACE AT THE RIGHT.*

Questions 1-9.

DIRECTIONS: Questions 1 through 9 are based on the sketch below showing one of the track rails on a section of track (pictured looking down on the track). The track rail rests directly on a tie plate at each tie and is fastened to each tie by spikes. The rail braces are placed over the tie plates. Errors on the track section incorrectly installed are to be determined by comparison with the section properly installed.

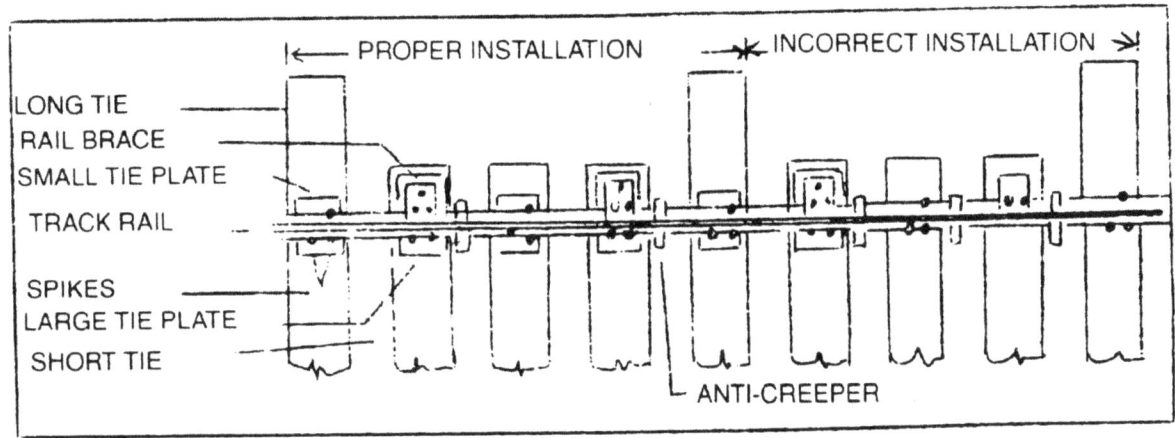

1. The properly installed section of track shows that only three spikes are used on every   1.____

   A. short tie   B. long tie
   C. anti-creeper   D. large tie plate

2. The properly installed section of track shows an equal number of small tie plates and   2.____

   A. long ties   B. short ties
   C. large tie plates   D. rail braces

3. The properly installed section of track shows the total number of spikes on the short ties is   3.____

   A. 6   B. 9   C. 13   D. 15

4. On the properly installed section of track, the total number of tie plates is   4.____

   A. 2   B. 3   C. 4   D. 5

5. The INCORRECTLY installed section of track has too many   5.____

   A. rail braces   B. anti-creepers
   C. small tie plates   D. large tie plates

6. The INCORRECTLY installed section of track has only ONE missing   6.____

   A. spike   B. large tie plate
   C. rail brace   D. small tie plate

23

7. To place the proper number of tie plates under the incorrectly installed section of track, the MINIMUM number of spikes which must be completely pulled out is

   A. 2   B. 6   C. 8   D. 10

8. On the incorrectly installed section of the track, the number of small tie plates missing is

   A. 1   B. 2   C. 3   D. 4

9. When the incorrectly installed section of track is completely corrected, then on this section of track, the total number of spikes will be

   A. 13   B. 14   C. 15   D. 16

Questions 10-17.

DIRECTIONS: Questions 10 through 17 are based on the sketch below showing a small section of track. Refer to this sketch when answering these questions.

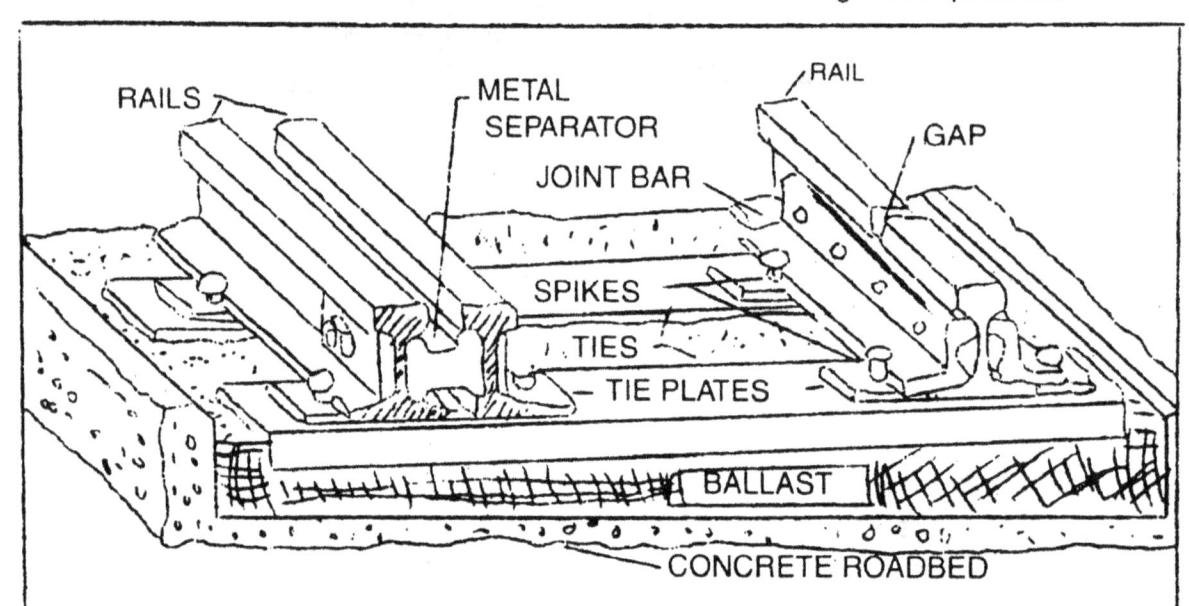

10. The MAIN purpose of the ballast is for

    A. absorbing heavy grease
    B. providing electrical insulation
    C. anchoring the spikes
    D. cushioning the ties

11. The single rail is higher than the double rail because the track is PROBABLY

    A. at a station   B. at a curve
    C. on a downgrade   D. on an upgrade

12. The extra rail shown acts as a(n) _____ rail.

    A. guard   B. power   C. signal   D. insulating

13. The fastenings through the joint bar and rail should be   13._____

    A. cut spikes   B. tapered pins
    C. rivets   D. bolts

14. The gap in the rail is provided to allow for rail   14._____

    A. vibration   B. expansion
    C. wear   D. settlement

15. The spacing between the two rails with the metal separator must be enough to allow   15._____
    space for the

    A. wheel flanges   B. ballast
    C. joint bar   D. tie plates

16. The PROPER order of assembly at the rail joint would be   16._____

    A. rails, spikes, joint bar   B. joint bar, spikes, rails
    C. rails, joint bar, spikes   D. spikes, rails, joint bar

17. Wood forms would be used for   17._____

    A. placing the ballast
    B. spacing the rails
    C. making the concrete roadbed
    D. spacing the ties

Questions 18-25.

DIRECTIONS: Questions 18 through 25 are based on the information contained in the safety rules given below. Read these rules carefully before answering these questions.

TRACKMEN SAFETY RULES ON EMERGENCY ALARM SYSTEM

In case of an emergency requiring the removal of high voltage power from the contact rail, any trackman seeing such emergency shall immediately operate the nearest emergency alarm box, and then immediately use the emergency telephone alongside the box to notify the trainmaster of the nature of the trouble. High voltage will be turned on again only by telephone order from an employee specifically having such authority. The location of this equipment along the trackway is indicated by a blue light. Trackmen are required to know the location of such boxes and the procedure to follow in order to have high voltage contact rail power removed on sections of elevated structure trackway which may not be equipped with emergency alarm boxes.

18. The location of an emergency alarm box is indicated by a(n) _____ light.   18._____

    A. red   B. orange   C. green   D. blue

19. Operating an emergency alarm box   19._____

    A. calls the fire department   B. removes power
    C. lights a blue light   D. restores power

20. All trackmen

    A. have the authority to have power restored
    B. should know the location of emergency alarm boxes
    C. must call the trainmaster before operating an emergency alarm box
    D. do not have the right to operate an emergency alarm box

21. On a track having trains in operation, a nearby emergency alarm box would PROBABLY be operated if

    A. an employee cuts his hand
    B. the emergency telephone rings
    C. the blue light is on
    D. a break is found in a running track rail

22. After operating an emergency alarm box, the trackman should use the emergency telephone immediately to speak to

    A. his supervisor
    B. the trainmaster
    C. the station agent
    D. his co-workers

23. It would be MOST important to have power restored as quickly as possible in order to reduce

    A. power waste
    B. train damage
    C. train delays
    D. fire hazard

24. If there are no emergency alarm boxes along a trackway, trackmen

    A. cannot have power shut off
    B. are not required to act in an emergency
    C. can have power shut off by following the proper procedure
    D. are forbidden to use the emergency telephone

25. On elevated structure trackways,

    A. emergency alarm boxes may not be found
    B. train delays never occur
    C. the trainmaster is not notified on power removal
    D. power is never removed

Questions 26-36.

DIRECTIONS: Questions 26 through 36 refer to the use of tools shown below. Read the question, and for the operation given, select the proper tool to be used from those shown. Print in the space at the right the letter given below your selected tool.

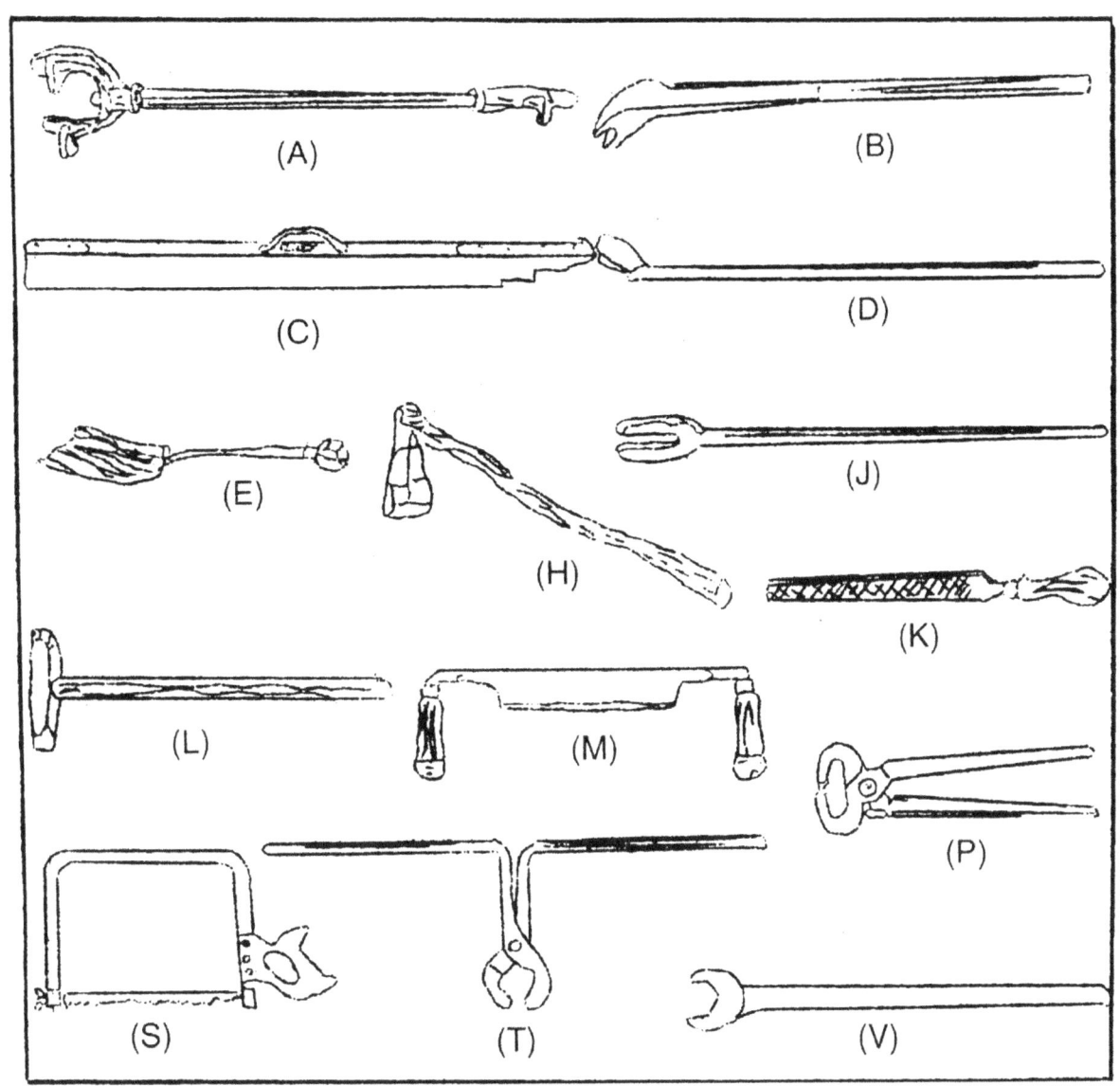

26. Driving a track cut spike (nail type) 26._____

27. Carrying a track rail 27._____

28. Checking the two rails of a track for difference in level 28._____

29. Tightening a track rail nut 29._____

30. Checking the distance separating the two rails of a track 30._____

31. Smoothing the rough edges of a track rail 31._____

32. Tamping or forcing rock ballast under a tie 32._____

33. Pulling out a track cut spike (nail type) 33._____

34. Cutting off a length of rail

35. Turning over an unfastened track rail

36. Trimming loose rock ballast between ties

37. Powdered lime is sometimes spread on certain sections of the roadway to

    A. soak up grease
    B. absorb moisture
    C. preserve the rails
    D. indicate a work area

38. Trackmen can BEST avoid accidents by

    A. knowing first aid
    B. working alone
    C. working fast
    D. being alert

39. A POOR procedure to follow when drilling is

    A. to use cutting oil when drilling metal
    B. tilting the drill sidewise to enlarge the hole
    C. tight clamping of the work
    D. setting the drill shaft tightly into the chuck

40. The MOST important reason for removing the handle from a jack left in the raised position under a piece of equipment is to avoid

    A. damage to the jack
    B. loss of the handle
    C. personal injury
    D. vibration of the handle

41. If a hole 1" in diameter is to be made in a steel rail, the BEST method to use is

    A. burning with an oxy-acetylene torch
    B. punching
    C. grinding
    D. drilling

42. The distance required for a train to make a full stop depends MOST on the

    A. width of the wheels
    B. type of car coupling
    C. condition of the wheels
    D. train speed

43. Gloves should be used for handling

    A. all small tools
    B. creosoted ties
    C. lanterns
    D. wooden rules

44. The BEST immediate first aid treatment for an eye burn caused by acid is to

    A. flush the eye with water
    B. bandage the eye
    C. dry the eye
    D. rub the eye

45. The advantage of track cut spikes (nail type) over track screw spikes is

    A. less rail damage
    B. better strength
    C. quicker installation
    D. less tie damage

46. A track rail would be shimmed to   46._____

    A. raise the rail   B. curve the rail
    C. make the rail flexible   D. loosen the rail

47. The BEST first aid treatment for a slight knee skin bruise would be   47._____

    A. a bandage and a splint
    B. a tourniquet
    C. washing and bandaging
    D. covering it with talcum powder

48. Tripper devices located on the subway roadway are for   48._____

    A. measuring train speed
    B. indicating a train is approaching
    C. automatically stopping trains
    D. preventing trackmen from falling

49. Rubber air hose is LEAST likely to become damaged when in prolonged contact with   49._____

    A. oil   B. water   C. grease   D. acid

50. The proper tool to use to make a 3/4" diameter hole through a wooden tie is a(n)   50._____

    A. reamer   B. round chisel
    C. auger   D. countersink

KEY (CORRECT ANSWERS)

1. B	11. B	21. D	31. K	41. D
2. B	12. A	22. B	32. D	42. D
3. C	13. D	23. C	33. B	43. B
4. D	14. B	24. C	34. S	44. A
5. B	15. A	25. A	35. J	45. C
6. B	16. C	26. L	36. E	46. A
7. C	17. C	27. T	37. A	47. C
8. B	18. D	28. C	38. D	48. C
9. D	19. B	29. V	39. B	49. B
10. D	20. B	30. A	40. C	50. C

TEST 5

DIRECTIONS: Each question or incomplete statement is followed by several suggested answers or completions. Select the one that BEST answers the question or completes the statement. *PRINT THE LETTER OF THE CORRECT ANSWER IN THE SPACE AT THE RIGHT.*

1. You would expect to find that subway track rails are made of

   A. copper   B. aluminum   C. steel   D. cast iron

2. The purpose of the bumping block at a dead-end track is to

   A. mark the end of the track
   B. prevent collision between two trains
   C. prevent a stopped train from rolling
   D. stop a train out of control

3. Subway trains are kept on the track by flanges on the wheels which bear on

   A. the outside of both rails
   B. both sides of both rails
   C. the inside of both rails
   D. the inside of one rail and the outside of the other

4. Track rails rest on wooden ties rather than directly on a concrete bed because the wooden tie

   A. raises the rail higher   B. gives added strength
   C. gives a softer ride   D. keeps the rail dry

5. Subway track rails usually come in 33' lengths. A good reason for NOT making them longer is

   A. the difficulty in handling
   B. that the rail may bend when carried
   C. that the fewer joints weaken the track
   D. that larger ties would be required

6. As a newly appointed man in a track gang, the assistant foreman will PROBABLY expect you to

   A. do more work than the others
   B. pay close attention to instructions
   C. make plenty of mistakes
   D. do all the dirty work

7. After several months' experience as a trackman, an older trackman cautions you that you are using a dangerous method. If you believe the method is faster and safe enough, you should

   A. assume that he has lost his nerve
   B. use your method but be careful
   C. suspect that he may be jealous of your progress
   D. follow his advice until you can check with the foreman

2 (#5)

8. One of the two track rails is sometimes installed higher than the other. You would expect to find this condition MOST often

   A. on curves
   B. in stations
   C. in storage yards
   D. on grades

9. The BEST first aid treatment to give a person who has stopped breathing is

   A. massage his chest
   B. a hot drink
   C. artificial respiration
   D. an application of cold compresses

10. Worn track rails are sometimes removed from main lines and reused in train storage yards PROBABLY because

    A. yard trains are empty and therefore lighter
    B. yards are seldom used
    C. the worn rail is lighter
    D. of the slow speed of trains in yards

11. The LEAST important information to be given to a newly appointed trackman would be

    A. train schedules
    B. the foreman to whom he is assigned
    C. safety instructions
    D. his working hours

12. If it is necessary to determine in the shop the number of large bolts loosely filling a large barrel without making a total count, the BEST procedure is to

    A. measure one bolt and measure the volume of the barrel
    B. count a small box full and measure the rest with the box
    C. weigh a few, weigh the barrel, weigh an empty barrel
    D. count one-tenth of the barrel and multiply by ten

13. The transit authority rules restrict the use of transit system telephones to official business.
    This means that these telephones should NOT be used by an employee to call

    A. a co-worker on a personal matter
    B. an ambulance for an injured passenger
    C. his superior for instructions
    D. the transit police in case of emergency

14. Trackmen often work in large gangs MAINLY because

    A. fewer foremen are required
    B. it helps morale
    C. many trades are involved
    D. the work is heavy and covers quite an area

15. Subway maps give information on train

    A. speeds
    B. time schedules
    C. routes
    D. delays

16. Many transit employees are given instructions in first aid.
    The MOST likely reason for this is to

    A. decrease the number of accidents
    B. interest the employees to call a doctor
    C. make it unnecessary to call a doctor
    D. provide temporary aid in case of an accident

17. A good procedure for a newly appointed inexperienced trackman to follow is to

    A. work fast to make a good first impression
    B. show interest in the work
    C. ask the foreman to repeat every instruction for safety
    D. be on the lookout for possible improvements in the work

18. When you are working in a large gang, it is MOST important that you

    A. do exactly the same amount of work as the others
    B. check the work of men near you
    C. do your particular assigned job properly
    D. help any man that needs help

19. It would be CORRECT to say that

    A. many safety rules are based on experience with past accidents
    B. carelessness is the cause of every accident
    C. accidents in dangerous work are excusable
    D. the majority of accidents are unavoidable

20. Tracks are constantly inspected by trackmen assigned as trackwalkers.
    From this it would be reasonable to believe that

    A. this continuous inspection is used to give experience to trackwalkers
    B. even a single defect may cause a serious accident
    C. many defects exist
    D. track construction is not very rugged

21. Tools should USUALLY be cleaned

    A. before use
    B. after use
    C. in spare time
    D. daily whether used or not

22. A steel track will shorten in length if the

    A. temperature increases   B. temperature decreases
    C. humidity increases   D. humidity decreases

23. When loosening a very tight nut with a long wrench, the GREATEST danger is

    A. blistering the hands   B. injuring a foot
    C. spraining the wrist   D. losing your balance

24. The LEAST likely result of a severe electric shock is 24.____
    A. bleeding
    B. stoppage of breathing
    C. a burn
    D. unconsciousness

25. To quickly remove the third rail power on any track, emergency switch boxes are provided along the tracks. One logical reason for operating the emergency box would be to 25.____
    A. prevent a train from hitting a trackwalker
    B. remove power in case of a fire on the track
    C. save power at night
    D. signal the motorman of an approaching train

26. When a gang of trackmen is working on the track, one man does nothing else but act as flagman to protect the gang. This procedure 26.____
    A. permits the rest of the gang to work effectively
    B. relieves the motorman of responsibility
    C. tends to place too much responsibility on one man
    D. tends to waste time

27. If a trackman working with his foreman near a subway station notices a large puddle of oil on the platform, the trackman should 27.____
    A. clean up the oil
    B. assume that the station porter will take care of it
    C. call it to the attention of his foreman
    D. locate the source of the oil

Questions 28-35.

DIRECTIONS: Questions 28 through 35 are based on the information contained in the trackmen duties given below. Read these duties carefully before answering these questions.

TRACKMEN DUTIES

Trackmen will report to and receive orders from assistant foremen of track. Trackmen will install, inspect, repair, replace, and maintain tracks, ties, ballast, track rail fastenings, and track rail electrical insulating joints. Additional duties of trackmen include clearing of tracks in case of accidents, snow removal, and tamping of ballast. Further duties of trackmen include such work in train storage yards or on road tracks, within the qualifications of their position, as their superiors may direct.

28. Trackmen receive their orders 28.____
    A. only from a foreman of track
    B. from either an assistant foreman or a foreman of track
    C. only from an assistant foreman of track
    D. from any foreman

29. A probable reason for assigning trackmen to snow removal is because

   A. trackmen cannot do their regular work when it snows
   B. snow removal is heavy work
   C. trackmen can make any necessary repairs at the same time
   D. tracks in yards and on elevated lines must be cleared of snow

30. Inspection of track rails is

   A. performed only by foremen
   B. only done after accidents
   C. the only inspection work performed by a trackman
   D. only one important duty of the trackman

31. A trackman's duties on trackwork do NOT include

   A. replacing track
   B. installing ties
   C. installing insulated joints
   D. repairing station platforms

32. The duties statement shows that trackmen MUST

   A. do any assigned work in connection with track
   B. often act as supervisors
   C. be able to do any work in the subway
   D. do other work when there is no trackwork

33. Tamping is a job USUALLY done in connection with

   A. inspection of insulated joints
   B. ballast work
   C. repair of rail fastenings
   D. snow removal

34. The rail fastenings which trackmen repair are for the

   A. third rail   B. track rails
   C. turnstile railings   D. station platform railings

35. The track rail insulated joints are designed to provide _____ insulation.

   A. electrical   B. heat
   C. sound   D. vibration

Questions 36-44.

DIRECTIONS: Questions 36 through 44 are based on the following sketch showing a pile of track ties. Refer to this sketch when answering these questions.

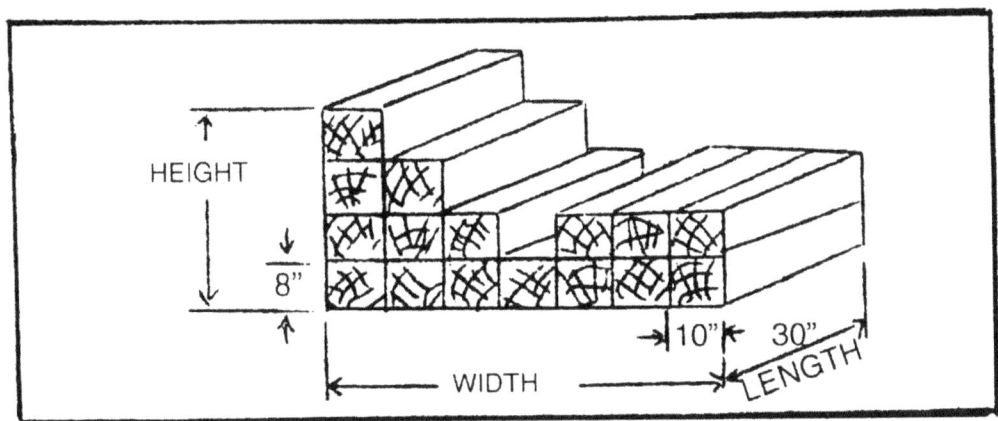

36. The total number of ties shown is 36.____
    A. 15   B. 16   C. 17   D. 18

37. The MAXIMUM height of the pile is 37.____
    A. 8"   B. 24"   C. 32"   D. 40"

38. The LOWEST height of any part of the pile is 38.____
    A. 8"   B. 10"   C. 16"   D. 32"

39. The pile is GREATER in _____ than in _____. 39.____
    A. length; width   B. height; width
    C. length; height   D. height; length

40. If all the ties shown are rearranged into a solid pile with an even height of 32" (4 ties high), then the new pile will be _____ ties wide. 40.____
    A. 6   B. 5   C. 4   D. 3

41. The total number of ties which do NOT rest directly on the ground is 41.____
    A. 7   B. 8   C. 9   D. 10

42. The size of each tie is 42.____
    A. 8" x 8" x 3'0"   B. 10" x 10" x 2'6"
    C. 8" x 10" x 2'6"   D. 10" x 8" x 3'0"

43. The ties shown are to be rearranged into a pile four ties high and four ties wide by moving as few ties as possible. The number of ties moved will be 43.____
    A. 6   B. 7   C. 8   D. 9

44. An equal number of blocks 8" x 10" x 3" and 8" x 10" x 4" are to be cut from one tie. The total number of each size block will be 44.____
    A. 9   B. 8   C. 6   D. 4

45. Grease on the track rails is MOST likely to cause

   A. derailment of trains
   B. wheel slippage when trains start or stop
   C. rusting of the rails
   D. rotting of ties

46. Lock washers are used on bolts fastening splice bars in place in order to

   A. make removal of the nuts easier
   B. avoid stripping the threads
   C. keep the bolts from turning
   D. prevent the nuts from loosening

47. Subway employees in general are forbidden to cross tracks from one platform to another unless absolutely necessary. The MAIN purpose of this rule is to

   A. avoid train delays
   B. prevent confusion
   C. protect the employee
   D. prevent interference with track work

48. By common sense, you would expect that the BEST way to move a lantern to stop a train is

   A. back and forth across the track
   B. straight up and down
   C. to and fro along the track
   D. in a circle over the head

49. In subway stations, a fixed narrow wooden strip is fastened to the train edge of the concrete platforms. The PROBABLE reason for this practice is to avoid

   A. damage to a swaying train and chipping of the concrete
   B. slipping by passengers alighting from trains
   C. large gaps between cars and platforms
   D. a sharp edge

50. An employee is not permitted to give a passenger a description of any lost article which he has found and turned in because

   A. employees are not permitted to hold long conversations with passengers
   B. this might aid the passenger to claim property not belonging to him
   C. this would delay the employee in his work
   D. the employee may make a mistake in the description

KEY (CORRECT ANSWERS)

1. C	11. A	21. B	31. D	41. C
2. D	12. C	22. B	32. A	42. C
3. C	13. A	23. D	33. B	43. A
4. C	14. D	24. A	34. B	44. D
5. A	15. C	25. B	35. A	45. B
6. B	16. D	26. A	36. B	46. D
7. D	17. B	27. C	37. C	47. C
8. A	18. C	28. B	38. A	48. A
9. C	19. A	29. D	39. D	49. A
10. D	20. B	30. D	40. C	50. B

EXAMINATION SECTION
TEST 1

DIRECTIONS: Each question or incomplete statement is followed by several suggested answers or completions. Select the one that BEST answers the question or completes the statement. *PRINT THE LETTER OF THE CORRECT ANSWER IN THE SPACE AT THE RIGHT.*

Questions 1-20.

DIRECTIONS: Questions 1 through 20, inclusive, refer to use of the proper tools, as illustrated on the last page, to perform certain tasks. Read each question and select the appropriate tool for the operation mentioned in the question in accordance with its identification number.

1. Two men carry a rail with No.
   A. 4   B. 26   C. 29   D. 39

2. Check difference in level between tracks with No.
   A. 9   B. 17   C. 28   D. 37

3. Spread rock ballast with No.
   A. 3   B. 4   C. 33   D. 44

4. Pull out rail spikes with No.
   A. 4   B. 26   C. 39   D. 44

5. Use on flange and turn rail over with No.
   A. 24   B. 27   C. 39   D. 49

6. Tighten nuts on rail with No.
   A. 13   B. 23   C. 32   D. 49

7. Cut scrap rails quickly with No.
   A. 1   B. 7   C. 40   D. 42

8. Place concrete around ties with No.
   A. 3   B. 27   C. 33   D. 44

9. Loosen solidly packed dirt and gravel with No.
   A. 10   B. 11   C. 33   D. 39

10. Break up six inch concrete slab with No.
    A. 2   B. 5   C. 20   D. 30

11. Cut a tie in two with No.
    A. 1   B. 14   C. 40   D. 42

12. Check squareness of saw cut with No.
    A. 9   B. 12   C. 34   D. 37

13. Determine length of rail with No.
    A. 16   B. 17   C. 34   D. 38

14. Tighten screw spikes with No.
    A. 13   B. 23   C. 31   D. 32

15. Cut shallow groove across tie with No.
    A. 19   B. 20   C. 36   D. 43

16. Remove burrs with No.
    A. 8   B. 19   C. 22   D. 30

17. Measure distance from running rail to third rail with No.
    A. 17   B. 34   C. 37   D. 38

18. Cut off piece from third rail protection board with No.
    A. 1   B. 2   C. 14   D. 40

19. Lift rail to insert tie plate with No.
    A. 4   B. 27   C. 39   D. 44

20. Cut off a piece of rail with No.
    A. 1   B. 14   C. 40   D. 42

21. A rail laid parallel to the running rails of a track to keep derailed wheels on the ties is a _____ rail.
    A. guard   B. joint   C. knuckle   D. stock

22. The reason for making sure that the level of the ballast in a switch is sufficiently below the tops of the ties is that
    A. the switch may drain properly
    B. there is no danger of the switch being thrown by accident
    C. there is no danger that the switch cannot be thrown when necessary
    D. ballast particles will not be thrown around by traffic action to cause damage or injury

23. Heat-treated rails are used instead of the ordinary steel rails on some portions of the transit system because they
    A. wear better
    B. are easier to drill
    C. have a lower initial cost
    D. are not affected by cold weather

24. The bolts on track joints should be tightened 24._____

   A. as much as possible
   B. with a short-handled wrench
   C. just enough so that the rails can expand and contract
   D. only a very slight amount to prevent damaging the spring washers

25. The MAIN purpose of giving employees instructions in first aid is to 25._____

   A. reduce the number of accidents
   B. save money on compensation cases
   C. eliminate the need for calling doctors
   D. be able to provide emergency aid if needed

26. A trackman working in a shop who is assigned to service the mechanical equipment used on trackwork should be capable of making repairs rapidly MAINLY because 26._____

   A. time between trains is short
   B. he gets paid more than the other men
   C. he is more experienced than the operators
   D. idle equipment results in decreased production

27. When a flagman signals the motorman to stop his train, the motorman should acknowledge the signal by 27._____

   A. one short blast of the whistle
   B. two short blasts of the whistle
   C. two long blasts of the whistle
   D. one long and one short blast of the whistle

28. In using a crane to place track panels on an elevated structure, it is considered good practice to have the crane operator take operating signals from only one person MAINLY because this 28._____

   A. requires fewer men
   B. avoids conflicting signals
   C. allows proper training of the signalman
   D. relieves the crane operator of all responsibility

29. When a motorman's view is limited on a curve, the flagging rules require that 29._____

   A. the hand trip should be placed farther away
   B. the flagman should be farther away from the work area
   C. a second set of flags should be placed before the first set
   D. only one set of flags should be used, but they should be placed farther away

30. The MAIN reason for having a small space between the ends of adjacent rails is that 30._____

   A. new rails are easier to install
   B. the space prevents electricity from flowing continuously in the rail
   C. the rails are easier to align
   D. the rails expand and contract as the temperature changes

31. The MOST important reason why a trackman should make sure that he does not leave a tool behind on the track after a job has been completed is that the tool   31.____

    A. will probably be needed on a similar job
    B. is his financial responsibility
    C. could cause an accident
    D. may be an expensive item to replace

32. It was estimated that a certain track concreting job would require 40 cubic yards of concrete. Actually the job took 38 1/2 cu.yds.   32.____
The percentage error from the estimate is MOST NEARLY

    A. 2%   B. 4%   C. .6%   D. 8%

33. The sum of 3'2 1/4", 0'8 7/8", 2'9 3/4", and 1'0" is   33.____

    A. 7'8 7/8"   B. 7'9"   C. 8' 7/8"   D. 15' 7/8"

34. If you are using an electric power tool which operates on third rail power, you should   34.____

    A. connect the negative lead to the signal rail
    B. connect the negative lead to the third rail
    C. connect the positive lead before connecting the negative lead
    D. disconnect the positive lead before disconnecting the negative lead

35. The MOST likely reason why a trackman should make out a report after using the contents of a first aid kit is that   35.____

    A. a new seal may be provided   B. the proper charge may be made
    C. used material may be replaced   D. unauthorized use may be prevented

36. A storage bin for rock ballast is 8'0" wide by 6'6" high by 22'0" long.   36.____
The volume of ballast, in cubic feet, that this bin can hold is MOST NEARLY

    A. 1058   B. 1082   C. 1116   D. 1144

37. The weight per foot of a length of square steel bar having a cross-section 1" x 1", as compared with one 1/2" x 1/2" in cross-section, is _____ times as much.   37.____

    A. 4   B. 3   C. 2 1/2   D. 2

38. According to the rules and regulations, the distance between caution lights or flags and the place at which the flagman is stationed must be at least _____ feet.   38.____

    A. 75   B. 200   C. 500   D. 1000

39. Pouring water on a track drill bit when drilling holes in a rail   39.____

    A. prevents warping of the holes
    B. prevents warping of the bolts
    C. preserves the temper of the rail steel itself
    D. preserves the temper of the drill's cutting edge

40. The number 0.085 can also be expressed as 85   40.____

    A. tenths   B. hundredths   C. thousandths   D. ten-thousandths

5 (#1)

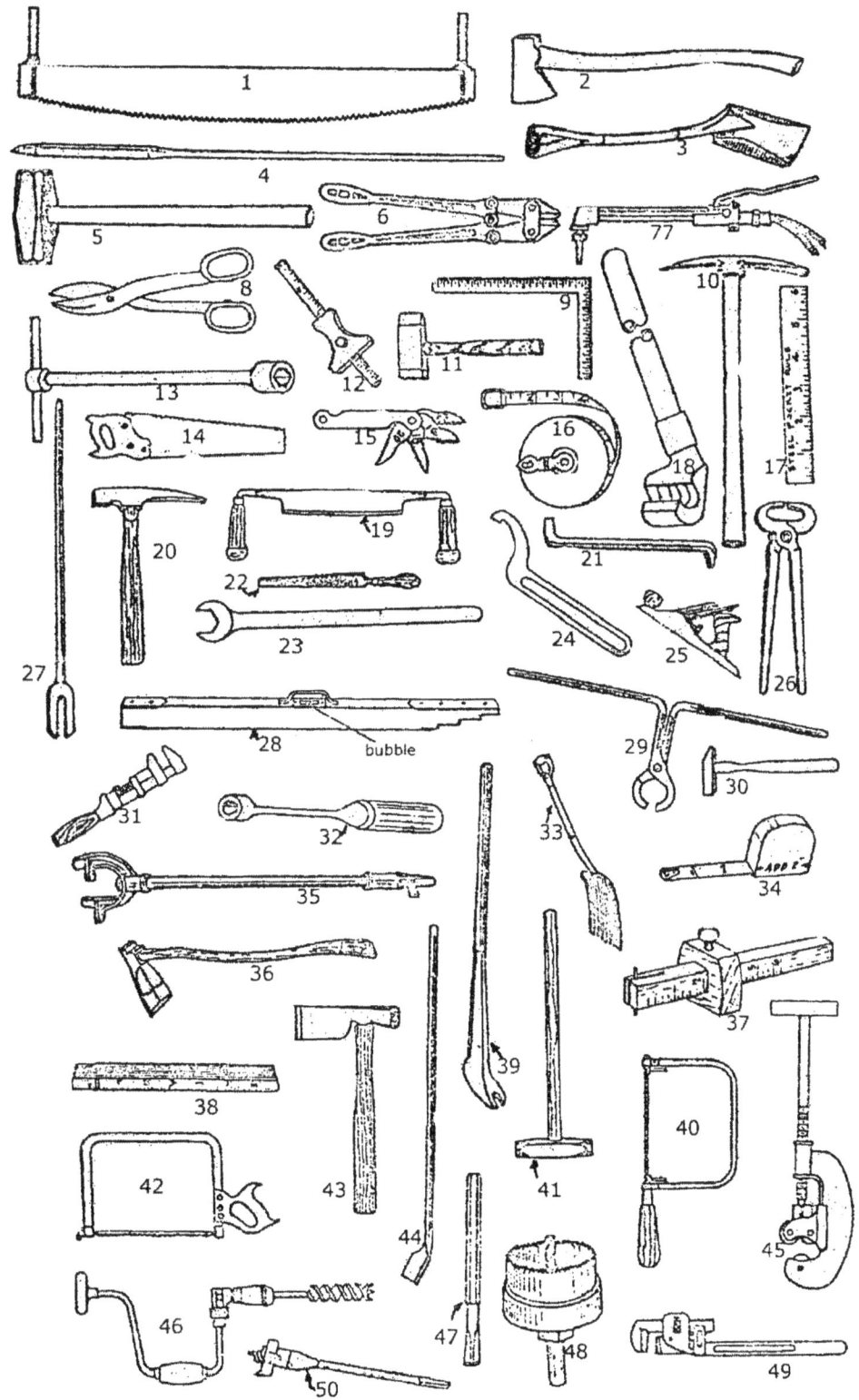

43

KEY (CORRECT ANSWERS)

1. C	11. A	21. A	31. C
2. C	12. A	22. C	32. B
3. C	13. A	23. A	33. A
4. C	14. A	24. C	34. D
5. B	15. C	25. D	35. C
6. B	16. C	26. D	36. D
7. B	17. D	27. B	37. A
8. A	18. C	28. B	38. C
9. A	19. D	29. C	39. D
10. B	20. D	30. D	40. C

TEST 2

DIRECTIONS: Each question or incomplete statement is followed by several suggested answers or completions. Select the one that BEST answers the question or completes the statement. *PRINT THE LETTER OF THE CORRECT ANSWER IN THE SPACE AT THE RIGHT.*

1. Of the following, the MAIN purpose of a safety training program is to

   A. fix the blame for accidents
   B. describe accidents which have occurred
   C. make the men aware of the basic causes of accidents
   D. maintain job progress under unsafe working conditions

2. The MOST important reason for training employees is to

   A. satisfy their ego
   B. satisfy the unions
   C. improve the men's ability to do a good job
   D. keep the supervisory personnel on their toes

3. If a fellow trackman is not breathing after receiving a shock from the third rail, it is MOST important for you to

   A. wrap him in a blanket
   B. force some hot coffee into him
   C. avoid moving him
   D. start artificial respiration

4. Sharp-edged tools should not be carried in a trackman's pocket MAINLY because the

   A. edge may become damaged
   B. tool is more readily lost
   C. tool may injure the trackman
   D. trackman may take the tool back to the locker room

5. Creosoted wood ties are preferred over plain wood ties because they

   A. hold spikes better
   B. stop track fittings from rusting
   C. give better protection against weathering
   D. have a hard surface which eliminates damage to ties by careless handling

6. Employees are directed not to make any statements concerning subway accidents except to proper officials, MAINLY because this will

   A. prevent lawsuits
   B. encourage passengers to feel safe
   C. avoid conflicting stories
   D. prevent unofficial statements from being accepted as official

7. The PRINCIPAL reason for the rule, *In walking on the track, walk opposite to the direction of traffic,* is that the man on the track

A. need not be very careful
B. will be seen by the motorman
C. is more likely to see an approaching train
D. is better able to judge the speed of a train

8. Trackmen are cautioned not to wear loose-fitting clothing while working MAINLY because such clothing may

   A. interfere with their work
   B. give insufficient warmth
   C. catch on some projection of a passing train
   D. catch and tear easily on the rough ties and rails

8.____

9. When inspecting railroad track ties, the BEST of the following methods of indicating a tie that will have to be renewed is to mark the

   A. tie with a spot of paint
   B. tie with a chalk mark
   C. web of the rail directly above the tie with a spot of paint
   D. web of the rail directly above the tie with a chalk mark

9.____

10. The MAIN purpose of periodic inspection of track work is to

    A. keep the men busy between track renewals
    B. encourage the men to take better care of the track
    C. make the men familiar with all types of track work
    D. discover minor faults before they develop into serious ones

10.____

11. In order to permit higher operating speeds on curves,

    A. the rail joints are made extra-tight
    B. a larger rail section is used on the outer rail
    C. the guard rail is double-spiked
    D. the outer rail is superelevated

11.____

12. The tool with which to slightly enlarge a bolt hole in a rail web would be a(n)

    A. cold chisel   B. drift pin
    C. auger bit   D. reamer

12.____

13. The distance covered in four minutes by a subway train traveling at 30 MPH is _____ mile(s).

    A. 1   B. 1 1/2   C. 2   D. 3

13.____

14. The jaws of a vise close 3/16" for each turn of the screw. If the vise is open 6 inches, the number of turns to close the jaws completely is

    A. 29   B. 30   C. 31   D. 32

14.____

15. The factor which is LEAST likely to make a trackman accident prone is

    A. job seniority   B. moonlighting
    C. poor health   D. job dissatisfaction

15.____

16. It is the PRIMARY function of tie plates to 16.____

    A. prevent the rail from creeping
    B. protect the rail against mechanical wear
    C. protect the ties against mechanical wear
    D. prevent the ties from slewing

17. The MOST serious defect which could result from improper handling of a spike maul when driving spikes would be 17.____

    A. nicking the rail
    B. breaking off the spike heads
    C. bending the spikes
    D. knocking the rail out of line

18. When cutting concrete with an air-operated hammer, it is MOST important to wear 18.____

    A. safety hats   B. safety shoes
    C. gloves   D. goggles

19. The hand signal which means *stop* is a light 19.____

    A. moved up and down
    B. rotated in a circular motion
    C. moved to and fro across the track
    D. held in a steady position in the center of the track

20. Portable train stops should be placed in the approach to a work area at a distance of AT LEAST _____ feet. 20.____

    A. 25   B. 75   C. 150   D. 500

Questions 21-30.

DIRECTIONS: Questions 21 through 30, inclusive, are based on the article about general safety precautions given below. In answering these questions, use ONLY the material in this article.

GENERAL SAFETY PRECAUTIONS

When work is being done on or next to a track on which regular trains are running, special signals must be displayed as called for in the general rules for flagging. Yellow caution signals, green clear signals, and a flagman with a red danger signal are required for the protection of traffic and workmen in accordance with the standard flagging rules. The flagman shall also carry a white signal for display to the motorman when he may proceed. The foreman in charge must see that proper signals are displayed.

On elevated lines during daylight hours, the yellow signal shall be a yellow flag, the red signal shall be a red flag, the green signal shall be a green flag, and the white signal shall be a white flag.

In subway sections, and on elevated lines after dark, the yellow signal shall be a yellow lantern, the red signal shall be a red lantern, the green signal shall be a green lantern, and the white signal shall be a white lantern.

Caution and clear signals are to be secured to the elevated or subway structure with non-metallic fastenings outside the clearance line of the train and on the motorman's side of the track.

21. On elevated lines during daylight hours, the caution signal is a 21.____

    A. yellow lantern B. green lantern
    C. yellow flag   D. green flag

22. In subway sections, the clear signal is a 22.____

    A. yellow lantern B. green lantern
    C. yellow flag   D. green flag

23. The MINIMUM number of lanterns that a subway track flagman should carry is 23.____

    A. 1   B. 2   C. 3   D. 4

24. The PRIMARY purpose of flagging is to protect the 24.____

    A. flagman   B. motorman
    C. track workers D. railroad

25. A suitable fastening for securing caution lights to the elevated or subway structure is 25.____

    A. copper nails B. steel wire
    C. brass rods   D. cotton twine

26. On elevated structures during daylight hours, the red flag is held by the 26.____

    A. motorman B. foreman C. trackman D. flagman

27. The signal used in the subway to notify a motorman to proceed is a 27.____

    A. white lantern B. green lantern
    C. red flag   D. yellow flag

28. The caution, clear, and danger signals are displayed for the information of 28.____

    A. trackmen B. workmen C. flagmen D. motormen

29. Since the motorman's cab is on the right-hand side, caution signals should be secured to the 29.____

    A. right-hand running rail
    B. left-hand running rail
    C. structure to the right of the track
    D. structure to the left side of the track

30. In a track work gang, the person responsible for the proper display of signals is the 30.____

    A. track worker B. foreman
    C. motorman   D. flagman

Questions 31-40.

DIRECTIONS: Questions 31 through 40, inclusive, refer to the track drawing shown below. In answering these questions, refer to this drawing.

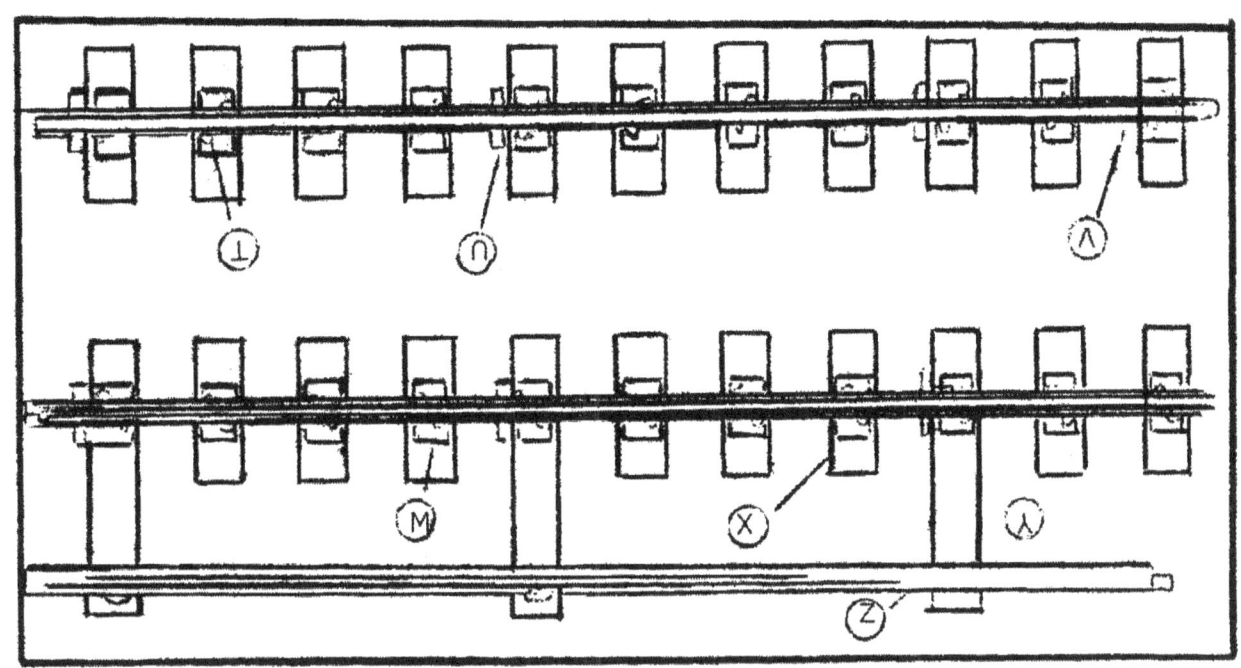

31. Ⓩ carries the

    A. power
    B. train coupling
    C. signals
    D. wheels

32. Ⓨ supports the

    A. ballast
    B. third rail
    C. signals
    D. guard rail

33. Ⓧ is used MAINLY to

    A. transmit load
    B. raise track
    C. eliminate bumps
    D. join rails

34. Ⓜ is a _____ tie.

    A. long   B. short   C. signal   D. switch

35. Ⓜ is made of

    A. concrete   B. steel   C. ballast   D. wood

36. Ⓜ has a length of APPROXIMATELY _____ ft.

    A. 1   B. 2   C. 4   D. 6

37. Ⓦ is a _____ plate.

    A. gusset   B. tie   C. splice   D. joint

38. Ⓥ is a _____ rail.

    A. running B. guard C. third D. mono

39. Ⓘ is a(n)

    A. rail stop
    B. rail joint
    C. insulated joint
    D. anti-creeper

40. Ⓣ has a length of APPROXIMATELY _____ in.

    A. 3/4 B. 2 C. 4 D. 6

KEY (CORRECT ANSWERS)

1. C	11. D	21. C	31. A
2. C	12. D	22. B	32. B
3. D	13. C	23. B	33. A
4. C	14. D	24. C	34. B
5. C	15. A	25. D	35. D
6. D	16. C	26. D	36. B
7. C	17. A	27. A	37. B
8. C	18. D	28. D	38. A
9. A	19. C	29. C	39. D
10. D	20. B	30. B	40. D

EXAMINATION SECTION
TEST 1

DIRECTIONS: Each question or incomplete statement is followed by several suggested answers or completions. Select the one that BEST answers the question or completes the statement. *PRINT THE LETTER OF THE CORRECT ANSWER IN THE SPACE AT THE RIGHT.*

Questions 1-8.

DIRECTIONS: Questions 1 through 8 are based on the sketch below showing one of the track rails on a section of track (as you would see it if you were standing on the track looking down). The track rail rests directly on a tie plate at each tie and is fastened to each tie by spikes. The rail braces are placed over the tie plates.

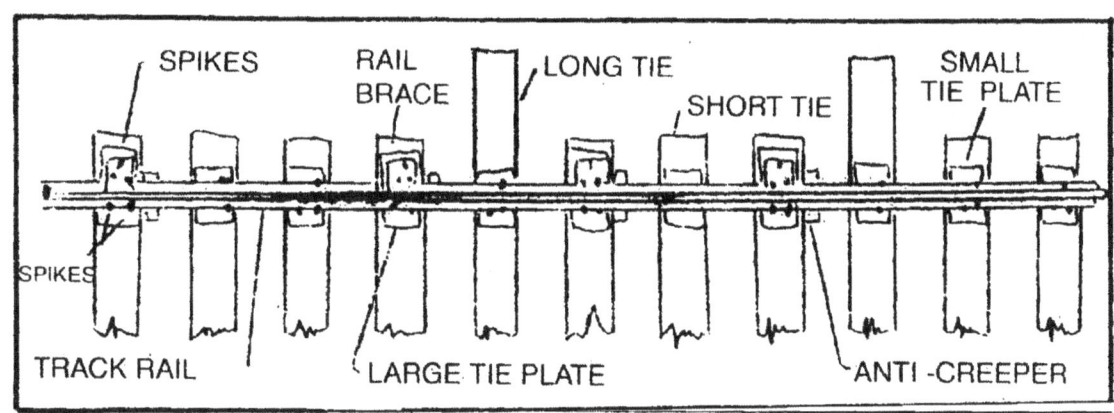

1. The sketch shows no spikes are used to hold the

   A. rail
   B. rail brace
   C. anti-creeper
   D. tie plate

   1.____

2. Anti-creepers are shown used at

   A. all long ties
   B. all short ties
   C. every other tie
   D. short ties with rail braces

   2.____

3. The sketch shows that the number of large tie plates is equal to the number of

   A. long ties
   B. rail braces
   C. small tie plates
   D. short ties

   3.____

4. As shown, a steel tie plate is always used between the rail and the wooden tie. The MOST likely purpose for the tie plate is to keep the rail from _____ the tie.

   A. bending at
   B. slipping on
   C. cutting into
   D. rotting

   4.____

5. The sketch shows that 5 spikes are used on every

   A. large tie plate
   B. long tie
   C. short tie
   D. small tie plate

   5.____

6. In driving the spikes through the small tie plate, it is reasonable to expect that the GREATEST danger would be in hitting the

   A. rail   B. tie plate   C. tie   D. ground

7. The total number of spikes shown is

   A. 20   B. 21   C. 40   D. 41

8. Rail braces are used wherever it is necessary to brace the rail sideways. Therefore, you would expect that rail braces would be used MOST commonly

   A. on grades
   B. on curves
   C. at stations
   D. on straight track

Questions 9-17.

DIRECTIONS: Questions 9 through 17 are based on the following sketch showing a track tie with instructions for drilling holes in the tie. Refer to this sketch when answering these questions.

INSTRUCTIONS FOR DRILLING HOLES IN TRACK TIES

◎ shows a 1" diameter hole to be drilled completely through the tie

○ shows a 3/4" diameter hole to be drilled to a depth of 5 1/2"

✕ shows a 1/2" diameter hole to be drilled to a depth of 4"

9. The total number of holes to be drilled down to 1/2" from the bottom of the tie is

   A. 1   B. 2   C. 5   D. 9

10. The diameter of the holes to be drilled completely through the tie is

    A. 1/2"   B. 3/4"   C. 1"   D. 6"

11. The 4" diameter holes are to be drilled _____ deep.

    A. 2"   B. 4"   C. 5 1/2"   D. 6"

12. The total number of holes to be drilled down a depth of 4" is

    A. 1   B. 2   C. 9   D. 12

13. The number of different auger bits required to drill all the holes is

    A. 3   B. 4   C. 5   D. 6

14. The holes that are MOST likely used to anchor-bolt the tie to the concrete roadway are shown by the symbol 14.____

   A. ✕
   B. ◎
   C. ○
   D. both ✕ and ◎

15. To properly drill part way through the tie, the BEST procedure is to 15.____

   A. cut the drill bit to the proper length
   B. mark the side of the tie
   C. keep lifting the drill bit from the hole
   D. clamp a stop on the drill bit

16. The holes to be drilled completely through the tie will be _____ deep. 16.____

   A. 4"   B. 5 1/2"   C. 6"   D. 10"

17. The MAXIMUM number of holes that can be drilled in the tie without changing drill-bits is 17.____

   A. 5   B. 6   C. 9   D. 10

Questions 18-25.

DIRECTIONS: Questions 18 through 25 are based on the information contained in the safety rules given. Read these rules carefully before answering these questions.

SAFETY RULES FOR EMPLOYEES WORKING ON TRACKS

Always carry a hand lantern whenever walking a track and walk opposite to the direction of the traffic on that particular track, if possible.

At all times when walking track, take note of and be prepared to use the spaces available for safety, clear of passing trains. Be careful to avoid those positions where clearance is insufficient.

Employees are particularly cautioned with respect to sections of track on which regular operation of passenger trains may at times be abandoned and which are used as lay-up tracks. Such tracks are likely to be used at any and irregular times by special trains such as work trains, lay-up trains, etc. At no time can any section of track be assumed to be definitely out of service and employees must observe, when on or near tracks, the usual precautions regardless of any assumption as to operating schedules.

18. Safety rules are MOST useful because they 18.____

   A. make it unnecessary to think
   B. prevent carelessness
   C. are a guide to avoid common dangers
   D. make the workman responsible for any accident

19. A trackman walking a section of track should walk   19._____

    A. to the left of the tracks
    B. to the right of the tracks
    C. in the direction of traffic
    D. opposite to the direction of traffic

20. One precaution a trackman should always take is to   20._____

    A. have power turned off on those tracks where he is walking
    B. place a red lantern behind him when walking back
    C. wave his lantern constantly when walking track
    D. note nearby safety spaces

21. Special trains are generally   21._____

    A. passenger trains on regular schedule
    B. express trains on local tracks
    C. work trains or lay-up trains
    D. trains going opposite to traffic

22. A trackman walking track should   22._____

    A. stay clear of all safety spaces
    B. expect all trains to be on schedule
    C. avoid tracks used by passenger trains
    D. carry a hand lantern

23. On sections of track not used for regular passenger trains, a trackman should   23._____

    A. follow the rules governing tracks in passenger train operation
    B. assume that no trains will be operating
    C. walk in the direction of traffic
    D. disregard the usual precautions

24. Safety spaces are provided in the subway for   24._____

    A. lay-up trains   B. passing trains
    C. employee's use   D. easier walking

25. A trackman would NOT expect lay-up tracks to be used by   25._____

    A. special trains   B. trains carrying passengers
    C. work trains   D. lay-up trains

Questions 26-36.

DIRECTIONS: Questions 26 through 36 refer to the use of tools shown below. Read the question, and for the operation given, select the proper tool to be used from those shown. Print the letter given below your selected tool in the space at the right.

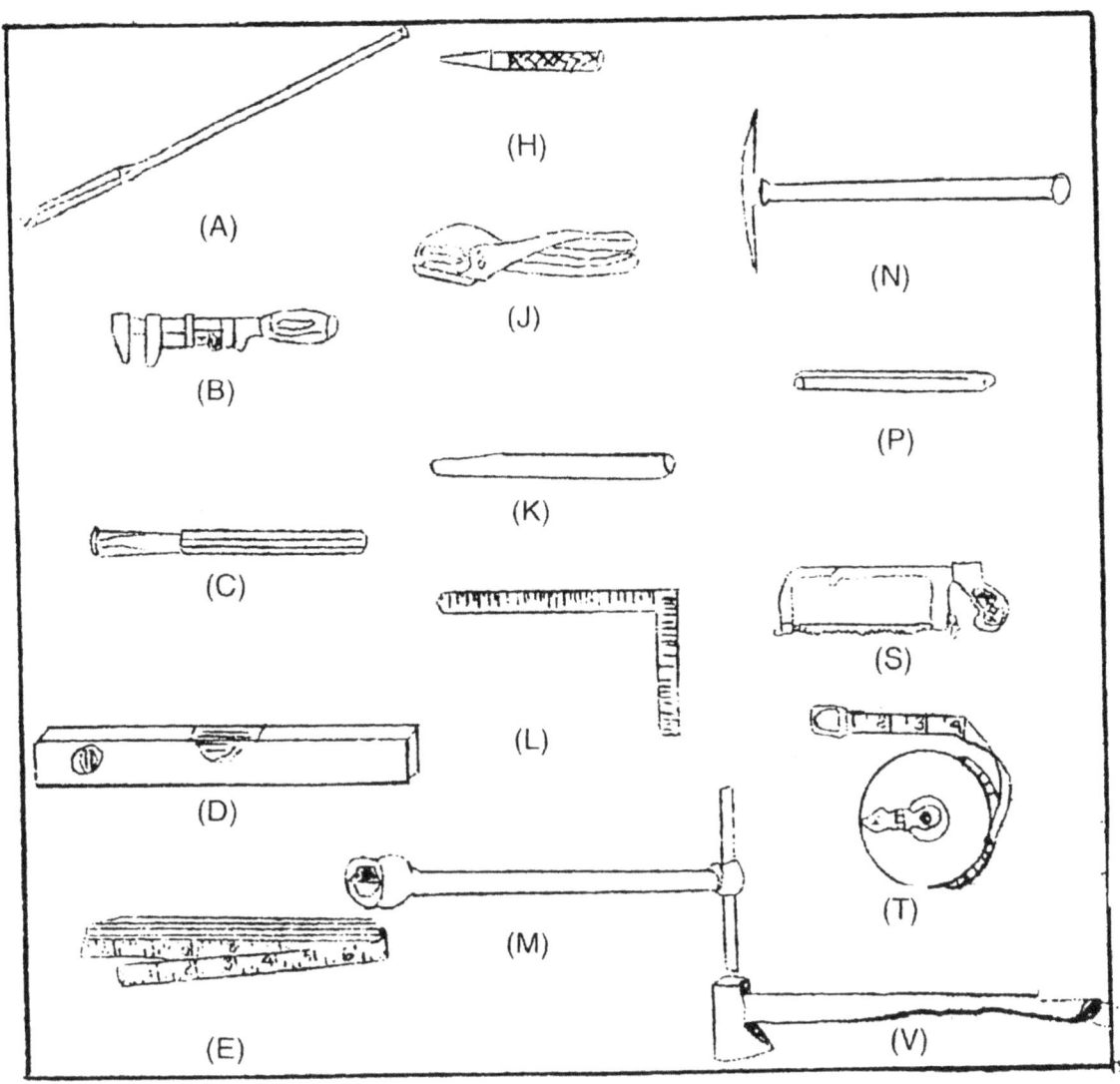

26. Lifting a track rail to insert a steel plate between tie and rail — 26._____
27. Drilling a shallow one-inch diameter hole in the concrete roadbed — 27._____
28. Cutting a piece from a 2" diameter steel rod — 28._____
29. Center-punching a steel plate before drilling a hole — 29._____
30. Checking the two rails of a track for level — 30._____
31. Tightening hexagon head screw spikes into a track tie — 31._____
32. Lining up holes in two heavy metal plates before inserting a bolt — 32._____
33. Making a half-twist in a 1/8" x 3/4" iron strap held in a vise — 33._____
34. Measuring the exact length of rail for a space approximately 30" long — 34._____
35. Removing a bolt rusted in place by knocking off the nut or head — 35._____
36. Cutting a shallow groove across a wooden tie — 36._____

Questions 37-43.

DIRECTIONS: Answer Questions 37 through 43 with reference to the accompanying diagram.

37. In order to pull the spike the rest of the way out, a small block should be placed at point

    A. 1
    B. 2
    C. 3
    D. 4

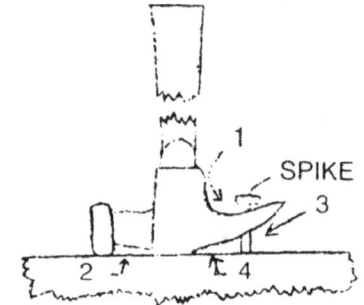

38. If the head of a sledge-hammer flies off when in the position shown, it will be thrown in direction

    A. 1
    B. 2
    C. 3
    D. 4

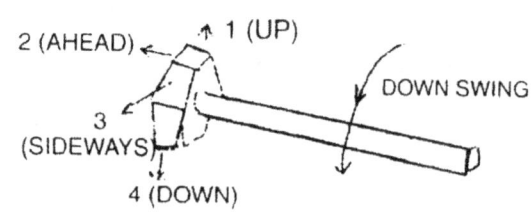

39. Four men are to carry a 15-foot rail. The BEST location of the men would be at points

    A. 1-2-3-4
    B. 2-3-6-7
    C. 1-3-5-7
    D. 1-4-5-8

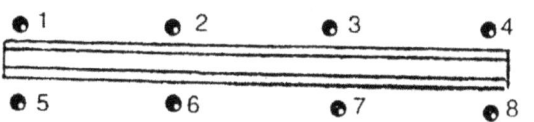

40. A fellow employee has been injured and is bleeding heavily at the knee. The BEST place to apply a tourniquet would be at point

    A. 1
    B. 2
    C. 3
    D. 4

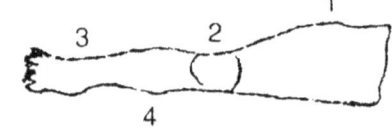

41. A trackman using the maul could strike the HARDEST blow if he held
    A. one hand near 1 and the other hand near 2
    B. both hands near 1
    C. both hands near 2
    D. one hand near 2 and the other hand near 3

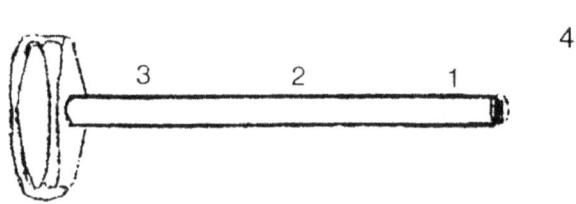

42. A trackman accidentally touching the third rail would be in the LEAST danger if he was standing on
    A. 1
    B. 2
    C. 3
    D. 4

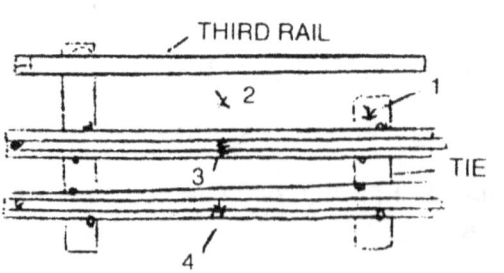

43. When replacing an old tie with a new one, the LAST piece put into place would be
    A. 1
    B. 2
    C. 3
    D. 4

44. Much of the replacement of track rails is done at night MAINLY because
    A. the tunnels are dark both day and night
    B. trains make better time at night
    C. many men prefer night work
    D. fewer trains run at night

45. Tools which are damaged should
    A. be used only for unimportant work
    B. be used if repairing them would be expensive
    C. never be used because you may be held responsible for the damage
    D. not be used because personal injury may result

46. A trackman on a station platform is accidentally bumped by a passenger and the passenger starts to scold him. The BEST procedure for the trackman to follow would be to
    A. tell the passenger to file a complaint with the railroad clerk
    B. try to prove it was the passenger's fault
    C. apologize and move away
    D. obtain the names of all witnesses to the affair

47. In the operation of the subways, it is always desirable to maintain good public relations. The opinion of the public would be LEAST affected by the
    A. attractiveness of subway posters
    B. kind of service rendered
    C. cleanliness of station platforms
    D. attitude of employees toward the public

48. When a train starts forward, the effect on the track is a tendency to
    A. spread the track
    B. push down on the track
    C. push the track forward
    D. push the track backward

49. If a trackman does not understand an order given to him by his foreman, he should
    A. look it up in the book of rules
    B. ask the foreman to explain it
    C. ask another trackman
    D. do the best he can

50. If a train on a certain route makes two round trips in 5 hours and 20 minutes, the average time for one round trip would be _____ hour(s) _____ minutes.

    A. 1; 20   B. 2; 30   C. 2; 40   D. 3; 10

KEY (CORRECT ANSWERS)

1. C	11. B	21. C	31. M	41. B
2. D	12. A	22. D	32. K	42. A
3. B	13. A	23. A	33. B	43. C
4. C	14. B	24. C	34. T	44. D
5. A	15. D	25. B	35. P	45. D
6. A	16. C	26. A	36. V	46. C
7. D	17. C	27. C	37. D	47. A
8. B	18. C	28. S	38. B	48. D
9. D	19. D	29. H	39. D	49. B
10. C	20. D	30. D	40. A	50. C

TEST 2

DIRECTIONS: Each question or incomplete statement is followed by several suggested answers or completions. Select the one that BEST answers the question or completes the statement. *PRINT THE LETTER OF THE CORRECT ANSWER IN THE SPACE AT THE RIGHT.*

1. Trains are LEAST likely to be delayed if a section of track is renewed   1.____

    A. in the morning   B. about noon
    C. in the evening   D. about midnight

2. When sand is delivered to a job for use in mixing concrete, it is GENERALLY measured in   2.____

    A. bushels   B. tons
    C. square yards   D. cubic yards

3. A strong foundation is needed under track ties because the ties   3.____

    A. are made of wood   B. must support a heavy load
    C. break easily   D. are very heavy

4. A trackman should NOT use a cold chisel, on which the head is badly beaten out of shape, because it   4.____

    A. will not cut   B. does not look good
    C. is dangerous   D. will bend

5. The GREATEST wear on the side of the rail head can be expected   5.____

    A. on curved tracks   B. on straight tracks
    C. at stations   D. on steep tracks

6. An employee is MOST likely to create a fire hazard by   6.____

    A. carrying a lighted lantern
    B. leaving piles of oily rags around the tracks
    C. sweeping dirt from platforms on to the tracks
    D. using paint around crowded station platforms

7. As the temperature increases, a steel rod becomes   7.____

    A. heavier   B. lighter   C. longer   D. shorter

8. A trackman should try to prevent accidents because MOST accidents are   8.____

    A. preventable   B. numerous
    C. fatal   D. frequently repeated

9. Tool boxes are used along the subway tracks for storage of tools and equipment. These boxes are provided so that tools will be   9.____

    A. dry when in use   B. safe when not in use
    C. used as little as possible   D. cleaned after being used

10. All trackmen in a crew should acquire at least a general knowledge of the tools and equipment assigned to their crew.
    The MOST likely reason for this is that each trackman

    A. may someday have to use them
    B. will become smarter than his foreman
    C. will do more work than the other trackman
    D. should know everything about the subway

11. If a passenger asks a subway employee for directions on how to reach a certain location, he should

    A. ignore the passenger
    B. refuse to answer
    C. answer the passenger politely
    D. never give such information

12. Subway employees are prohibited from engaging in horseplay while on the job MAINLY because it is

    A. childish   B. dangerous
    C. tiresome   D. unnecessary

Questions 13-23.

DIRECTIONS: Questions 13 through 23 in Column I are various products, used in the maintenance of the subway. Column II consists of materials commonly used for these products. For each item in Column I, select from Column II the proper material from which it is commonly made. Print the letter given beside the material you select for each question in the space at the right.

COLUMN I (Products)	COLUMN II (Materials)
13. Track rail	A. Copper
14. Subway tie	B. Glass
15. Track bolt	C. Asbestos
16. Bare electric wire	D. Steel
17. Concrete	E. Grease
18. Electric light globe	H. Wood
19. Track spike	J. Cement
20. Signal light lens	L. Canvas
21. Tarpaulin cover	
22. Lubricant	
23. Fireproof gloves	

24. The MAIN reason for constantly inspecting tracks is to

   A. keep them from getting rusty
   B. eliminate all noises
   C. prevent them from getting dirty
   D. find track defects quickly

25. Suppose you are called on to give first aid to several victims of an accident. First attention should be given to the one who is

   A. bleeding severely
   B. groaning loudly
   C. unconscious
   D. vomiting

26. Newly appointed trackmen should carry out the foremen's orders as they are given because the foremen

   A. are older
   B. are in charge of the work
   C. never make mistakes
   D. are more educated

27. A subway train approaching men working on the track warns then by

   A. blowing a whistle
   B. flashing its front lights on and off
   C. ringing a bell
   D. blowing a horn

28. A trackman should ordinarily expect a subway train approaching a sharp curve to

   A. stop
   B. speed up
   C. slow down
   D. continue at the same speed

29. In the subway, the color of a signal light commonly used to stop a train is

   A. red   B. yellow   C. orange   D. green

Questions 30-44.

DIRECTIONS: Questions 30 through 44 are based on the following figure. Each question indicates the proper figure to be used when answering the question. Figure 1 shows a stack of steel bars. Figure 2 shows a short tie with dimensions. Figure 3 shows a stack of long ties with dimensions.

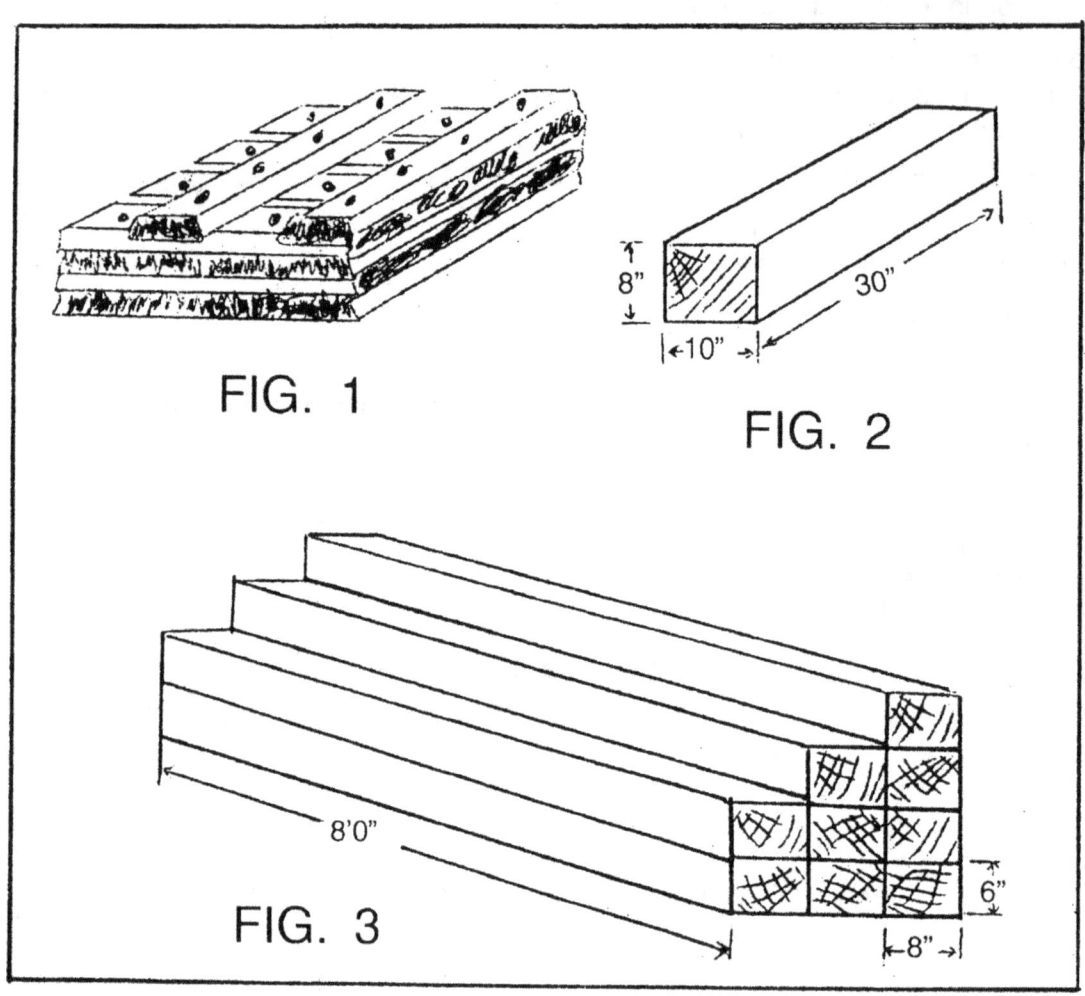

30. In Figure 1, the number of steel bars in the stack is

    A. 10   B. 12   C. 18   D. 20

31. In Figure 1, each steel bar is 1 1/2" thick. The GREATEST height of the stack is

    A. 4 1/2"   B. 6"   C. 7 1/2"   D. 9"

32. Two of the steel bars shown in Figure 1 are to be bolted together.
    If only half of the holes in the two bars are to be used, the number of bolts required is

    A. 1   B. 4   C. 6   D. 8

33. In Figure 1, each bar weighs 20 pounds.
    The weight of the entire stack of bars is _____ lbs.

    A. 100   B. 180   C. 200   D. 360

34. In Figure 1, the stack originally consisted of six layers, with four steel bars in each layer.
    The number of bars that were removed from the original stack is

    A. 2   B. 6   C. 10   D. 14

35. In Figure 1, the number of bars in contact with the floor is   35._____
    A. 4   B. 7   C. 8   D. 9

36. The length of the tie in Figure 2 is   36._____
    A. 2'   B. 2'3"   C. 2'6"   D. 3'

37. The number of faces (sides, ends, top, and bottom) on the tie in Figure 2 is   37._____
    A. 3   B. 4   C. 5   D. 6

38. In Figure 2, if the 8" dimension is the height of the tie, then the length of the tie is about   38._____
    _____ times the height.
    A. 2   B. 3 1/2   C. 4 1/2   D. 5

39. In Figure 3, the floor area occupied by the stack of ties is   39._____
    A. 24" x 8"   B. 24" x 98"   C. 2' x 8'   D. 24' x 8'

40. In Figure 3, the whole stack of ties was originally four ties high.   40._____
    The number of ties in the original stack was
    A. 4   B. 8   C. 12   D. 16

41. In Figure 3, if the ties are laid on edge, instead of flat, the volume of the stack will be   41._____
    A. smaller   B. the same
    C. twice as great   D. three times as great

42. In Figure 3, the height of the entire stack of ties is to be reduced to 12".   42._____
    The SMALLEST number of ties that have to be moved to do this is _____ tie(s).
    A. 1   B. 2   C. 3   D. 6

43. The number of planks, 3" x 6" x 8', that can be cut from one of the ties in Figure 3 is   43._____
    A. 2   B. 3   C. 4   D. 5

44. If all of the ties shown in Figure 3 were laid end to end to form a guard rail, the length of   44._____
    the guard rail would be
    A. 8'   B. 32'   C. 72'   D. 96'

45. Before stepping on a subway track, a trackman should   45._____
    A. see if the third rail has current in it
    B. look in each direction
    C. obtain a copy of the timetable
    D. always tell someone where he is going

46. If it becomes necessary to touch the third rail, a trackman should make sure it is not   46._____
    A. broken   B. carrying current
    C. grounded   D. loose

47. Before using an electric drill, a trackman should make sure it

    A. is in good condition
    B. has not been used by anyone else
    C. is not painted
    D. has just been overhauled

48. When walking along a subway track, it is preferable that a trackman should

    A. walk in the direction opposite to traffic
    B. walk on the rail
    C. never carry a lantern
    D. avoid subway stations

49. Trackmen should use a stop signal for approaching trains when the

    A. men are eating lunch
    B. trains travel too fast
    C. foreman is approaching
    D. men are changing a track rail

50. When a train is approaching, men on the tracks should

    A. start to work
    B. stop the train if the track is clear
    C. stand clear of the track
    D. make sure the motorman is not speeding

KEY (CORRECT ANSWERS)

1. D	11. C	21. L	31. C	41. B
2. D	12. B	22. E	32. A	42. C
3. B	13. D	23. C	33. D	43. A
4. C	14. H	24. D	34. B	44. C
5. A	15. D	25. A	35. A	45. B
6. B	16. A	26. B	36. C	46. B
7. C	17. J	27. A	37. D	47. A
8. A	18. B	28. C	38. B	48. A
9. B	19. D	29. A	39. C	49. D
10. A	20. B	30. C	40. C	50. C

TEST 3

DIRECTIONS: Each question or incomplete statement is followed by several suggested answers or completions. Select the one that BEST answers the question or completes the statement. *PRINT THE LETTER OF THE CORRECT ANSWER IN THE SPACE AT THE RIGHT.*

Questions 1-14.

DIRECTIONS: Questions 1 through 14 are based on the figures appearing below. Figure 1 shows a section of track including track rails and the third rail. The track rails rest directly on a tie plate at each tie and are fastened to each tie by two spikes. The third rail rests on porcelain insulators, instead of tie plates, and does not require any spikes. Long ties are used to support both the third rail and the outside track rail; the short ties support only the track rails. Figure 2 is the same section of track shown in Figure 1 but with certain parts intentionally omitted or misplaced for the purpose of this test.

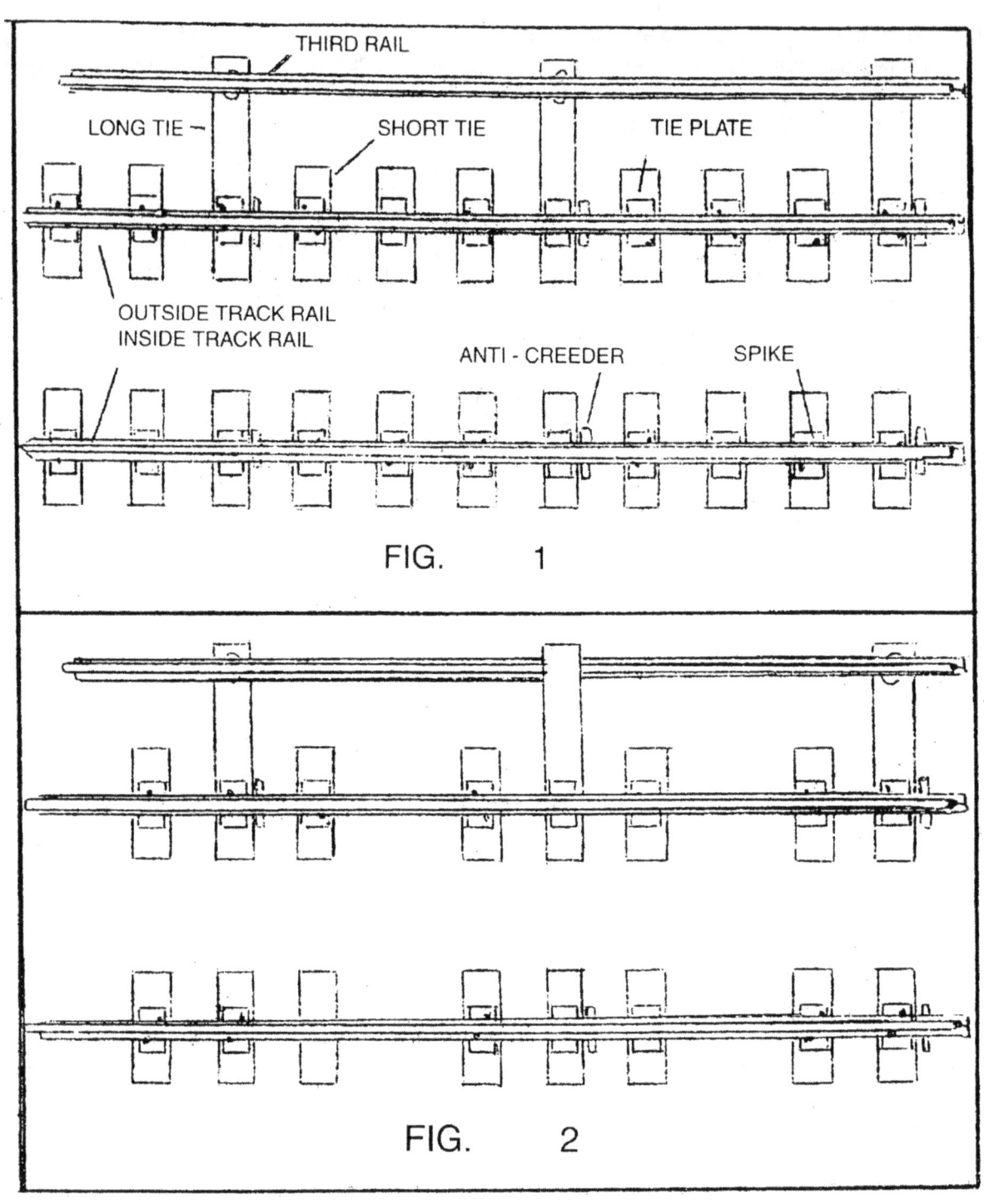

FIG. 1

FIG. 2

1. The total number of short ties shown in Figure 1 is

   A. 13   B. 16   C. 19   D. 22

2. The total number of spikes shown in Figure 1 is

   A. 32   B. 38   C. 44   D. 50

3. In Figure 1, there are 3._____

   A. less ties than tie plates
   B. as many ties as tie plates
   C. more ties than tie plates
   D. twice as many tie plates as there are ties

4. In Figure 1, long ties are used under 4._____

   A. the third rail and outside track rail
   B. the outside track rail only
   C. the third rail only
   D. both the inside and outside track rails

5. In Figure 1, anti-creepers are used next to 5._____

   A. long ties only
   B. short ties only
   C. all ties
   D. the long ties and some of the short ties

6. The number of different kinds of ties shown in Figure 1 is 6._____

   A. 2 B. 3 C. 4 D. 22

7. In Figure 1, the outside track rail rests directly on the 7._____

   A. short ties   B. long ties
   C. spikes   D. tie plates

8. A train on the track in Figure 1 would have its wheels riding on 8._____

   A. the inside track rail and the third rail
   B. the inside track rail and the outside track rail
   C. the outside track rail and the third rail
   D. all three rails

9. The total number of spikes missing from the track in Figure 2 is 9._____

   A. 12 B. 14 C. 16 D. 18

10. The total number of short ties missing from the track in Figure 2 is 10._____

    A. 2 B. 3 C. 4 D. 6

11. The total number of tie plates missing from the track in Figure 2 is 11._____

    A. 1 B. 4 C. 6 D. 7

12. One kind of item which is NOT missing in Figure 2 is a 12._____

    A. track rail   B. short tie
    C. tie plate   D. spike

13. The long tie which is IMPROPERLY installed in Figure 2 is shown 13._____

    A. on top of the third rail   B. too far to the right
    C. under the third rail   D. too far to the left

14. The tie shown IMPROPERLY installed in Figure 2 would
    A. not affect train operation
    B. not offer support for the third rail
    C. still support the third rail
    D. support the inside track rail but not the third rail

Questions 15-34.

DIRECTIONS: Questions 15 through 34 refer to operations involving the use of tools shown on the following page. Read each question and for the operation given, select the proper tool to be used from those shown on the following page. Print the letter given beside the tool you select for each question in the space at the right.

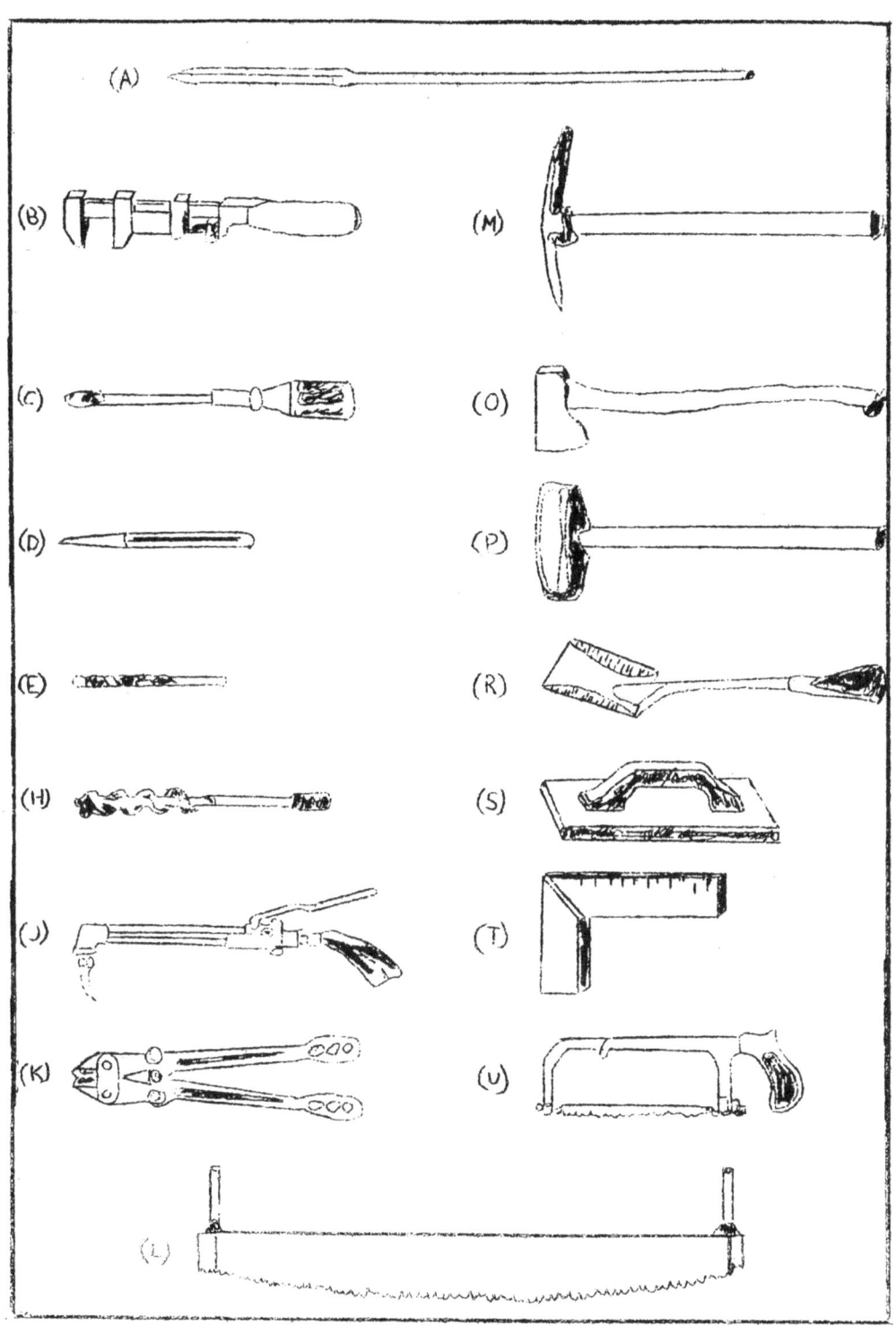

15. Sawing off the end of a bolt 15.____

16. Drilling a hole in a steel plate 16.____

17. Cutting scrap rail quickly into short lengths 17.____

18. Mixing concrete 18.____

19. Chopping off a piece of timber 19.____

20. Snipping off a piece of steel wire   20._____

21. Loading sand into a wheelbarrow   21._____

22. Loosening up a pile of solidly packed dirt and gravel   22._____

23. Drilling a large hole in a piece of timber   23._____

24. Breaking up a slab of concrete   24._____

25. Burning a hole in a piece of steel   25._____

26. Shifting a long piece of rail along the ground   26._____

27. Tightening a nut on a bolt   27._____

28. Making a straight cut through a heavy piece of timber   28._____

29. Inserting a round-head wood screw   29._____

30. Marking the center of a hole to be drilled in a steel plate   30._____

31. Determining if a piece of timber has been cut off squarely   31._____

32. Putting a smooth surface on concrete   32._____

33. Putting sharp points on the ends of wooden stakes   33._____

34. Measuring the thickness of a board   34._____

Questions 35-40.

DIRECTIONS: Questions 35 through 40, inclusive, are various types of injuries which would MOST likely result from careless use of the objects shown in the following picture. For the type of injury given in each question, select from the picture the object which MOST likely caused it. Print the letter given beside the object you select for each question in the space at the right.

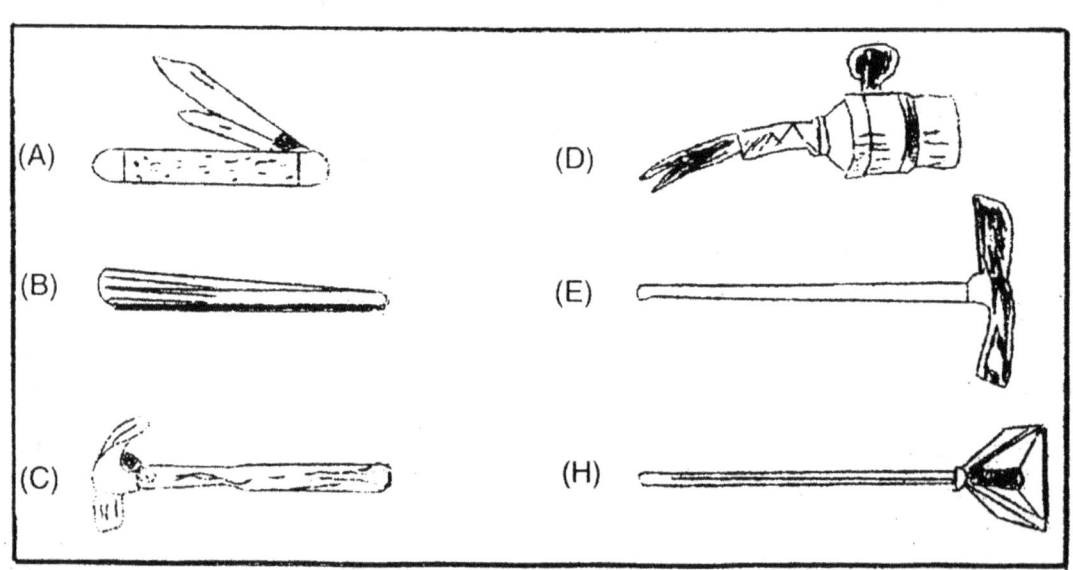

35. Bruised finger 35.____

36. Eye cut by concrete chip 36.____

37. Cut leg 37.____

38. Electric shock 38.____

39. Cut finger 39.____

40. Crushed toe 40.____

Questions 41-50.

DIRECTIONS: Questions 41 through 50 are based on the information contained in the following safety rules. Read the rules carefully before answering these questions.

SAFETY RULES

Employees must take every precaution to prevent accidents, or injury to persons, or damage to property. For this reason, they must observe conditions of the equipment and tools with which they work, and the structures upon which they work.

It is the duty of all employees to report to their superior all dangerous conditions which they may observe. Employees must use every precaution to prevent the origin of fire. If they discover smoke or a fire in the subway, they shall proceed to the nearest telephone and notify the trainmaster giving their name, badge number, and location of the trouble.

In case of accidents on the subway system, employees must, if possible, secure the name, address, and telephone number of any passengers who may have been injured.

Employees at or near the location of trouble on the subway system, whether it be a fire or an accident, shall render all practical assistance which they are qualified to perform.

41. The BEST way for employees to prevent an accident is to 41.____

    A. secure the names of the injured persons
    B. arrive promptly at the location of the accident
    C. give their name and badge numbers to the trainmaster
    D. take all necessary precautions

42. In case of trouble, trackmen are NOT expected to 42.____

    A. report fires
    B. give help if they don't know how
    C. secure telephone numbers of persons injured in subway accidents
    D. give their badge number to anyone

43. Trackmen MUST 43.____

    A. be present at all fires
    B. see all accidents
    C. report dangerous conditions
    D. be the first to discover smoke in the subway

44. Observing conditions means to
    A. look at things carefully
    B. report what you see
    C. ignore things that are none of your business
    D. correct dangerous conditions

45. A dangerous condition existing on the subway system which a trackman should observe and report to his superior would be
    A. passengers crowding into trains
    B. trains running behind schedule
    C. tools in defective condition
    D. some newspapers on the track

46. If a trackman discovers a badly worn rail, he should
    A. not take any action
    B. remove the worn section of rail
    C. notify his superior
    D. replace the rail

47. The MAIN reason a trackman should observe the condition of his tools is
    A. so that they won't be stolen
    B. because they don't belong to him
    C. to prevent accidents
    D. because they cannot be replaced

48. If a passenger who paid his fare is injured in a subway accident, it is MOST important that an employee obtain the passenger's
    A. name
    B. age
    C. badge number
    D. destination

49. An employee who happens to be at the scene of an accident on a crowded station of the system should
    A. not give assistance unless he chooses to do so
    B. leave the scene immediately
    C. question all bystanders
    D. render whatever assistance he can

50. If a trackman discovers a fire at one end of a station platform and telephones the information to the trainmaster, he need NOT give
    A. the trainmaster's name
    B. the name of the station involved
    C. his own name
    D. the number of his badge

KEY (CORRECT ANSWERS)

1. C	11. D	21. R	31. T	41. D
2. C	12. A	22. M	32. S	42. B
3. B	13. A	23. H	33. O	43. C
4. A	14. B	24. P	34. T	44. A
5. D	15. U	25. J	35. C	45. C
6. A	16. E	26. A	36. B	46. C
7. D	17. J	27. B	37. E	47. C
8. B	18. R	28. L	38. D	48. A
9. C	19. O	29. C	39. A	49. D
10. D	20. K	30. D	40. H	50. A

EXAMINATION SECTION
TEST 1

DIRECTIONS: Each question or incomplete statement is followed by several suggested answers or completions. Select the one that BEST answers the question or completes the statement. *PRINT THE LETTER OF THE CORRECT ANSWER IN THE SPACE AT THE RIGHT.*

1. Newly appointed trackmen should carry out the foremen's orders as they are given because the foremen

    A. are older
    B. are in charge of the work
    C. never make mistakes
    D. are more educated

    1.____

2. The MAIN reason a trackman should observe the condition of his tools is

    A. so that they won't be stolen
    B. because they don't belong to him
    C. to prevent accidents
    D. because they cannot be replaced

    2.____

3. An employee who happens to be at the scene of an accident on a crowded station of the system *should*

    A. hot give assistance unless he chooses to do so
    B. leave the scene immediately
    C. question all bystanders
    D. render whatever assistance he can

    3.____

4. The wrench which is LEAST likely to slip off a nut of standard size is a _____ wrench.

    A. chain   B. box   C. monkey   D. spanner

    4.____

5. An oilstone is LEAST likely to be used to sharpen a

    A. scraper   B. chisel   C. knife   D. saw

    5.____

6. Rubber tubing deteriorates most rapidly when in contact with

    A. water   B. air   C. oil   D. soapsuds

    6.____

7. The proper file to use for enlarging a small circular hole is a _____ file.

    A. rat-tail   B. flat   C. square   D. mill

    7.____

8. When using a hacksaw, it is *good* practice to

    A. tighten the blade by using pliers on the wing nut
    B. use heavy pressure on both the forward and return strokes
    C. slow the speed of cutting when the piece is almost cut through
    D. use very short, very rapid strokes

    8.____

9. A slight coating of rust on small tools is *best* removed by

   A. applying a heavy coat of vaseline
   B. scraping with a sharp knife
   C. rubbing with kerosene and fine steel wool
   D. rubbing with a dry cloth

10. A *good* reason for keeping a cold chisel free from oil or grease is to

    A. make it cut better
    B. avoid oil splattering from the blows
    C. prevent change in temper
    D. prevent the hammer from glancing off the chisel head

11. Cotter pins are most generally used with _____ nuts.

    A. acorn   B. castellated   C. knurled   D. wing

12. A trackman should NOT put his hand in the path of the discharge from a carbon dioxide fire extinguisher because the discharge

    A. is a poisonous liquid
    B. is very hot
    C. can be re-used
    D. can cause a frost-bite

13. Employees of the transit system are cautioned not to use water to extinguish electrical fires. The BEST reason for this rule is that water

    A. will cause the fuses to blow in the electrical circuits
    B. will cause corrosion of sensitive electrical parts
    C. coming into contact with a hot electrical arc causes asphyxiating fumes to be generated
    D. may conduct the electrical current and create a shock hazard

14. Engaging in horseplay while on the job is prohibited because it is

    A. dangerous   B. childish   C. tiresome   D. unnecessary

15. The distance between the rails on which the trains run is *nearest* to _____ feet.

    A. 2   B. 5   C. 8   D. 10

16. The edges of station platforms are made of

    A. cement   B. stone   C. metal   D. wood

17. Where the edges of station platforms are painted, the color is

    A. silver   B. red   C. green   D. yellow

18. The third rail is located

    A. to one side of the running rails
    B. between the running rails
    C. on the subway wall
    D. just under the subway roof

19. Signals which tell the motorman whether there is a train ahead are generally   19._____

   A. to the right of the track
   B. to the left of the track
   C. above the center of the track
   D. between the rails on the subway floor

20. The two materials which have been used to the greatest extent for construction of the   20._____
    subway system are

   A. steel and concrete   B. wood and steel
   C. concrete and brick   D. brick and stone

21. The width of subway cars is nearest to _____ feet.   21._____

   A. 5   B. 10   C. 15   D. 20

22. The walls of most subway local stations are faced with   22._____

   A. brick   B. marble   C. tile   D. cement

23. The difference in height between the bottom and top of a ten-step stairway is about   23._____
    _____ feet.

   A. 10   B. 8   C. 6   D. 4

24. Some subway stations are brighter than others because of the use of   24._____

   A. chrome   B. fluorescent lamps
   C. reflectors   D. spot lights

25. Tool boxes are used along the subway tracks for storage of tools and equipment.   25._____
    These boxes are provided so that tools will be

   A. in a safe location when not in use   B. dry when in use
   C. used as little as possible   D. cleaned after being used

26. Trackmen can *best* avoid accidents by   26._____

   A. being alert   B. working fast
   C. working alone   D. studying first-aid

27. Work gloves should be worn when handling   27._____

   A. lanterns   B. wooden ties
   C. pliers   D. electric drills

28. The BEST first-aid treatment for a slight knee skin bruise is   28._____

   A. massage   B. talcum powder
   C. a tourniquet   D. washing and bandaging

29. As a prime safety precaution, before stepping on a subway track a trackman should   29._____

   A. make sure the third rail is dead   B. notify his foreman
   C. look both ways   D. turn his lantern off

4 (#1)

30. As a newly appointed man in a track gang, the foreman will expect you to

    A. do more work than the others
    B. pay close attention to instructions
    C. make plenty of mistakes
    D. do all the dirty work

31. After several months' experience as a trackman, an older trackman cautions you that you are using a dangerous method. If you believe your method is faster and safe enough, you should

    A. assume that he has lost his nerve
    B. use your method but be careful
    C. suspect that he may be jealous of your progress
    D. follow his advice until you can check with the foreman

32. The BEST first-aid treatment to give a person who has stopped breathing is

    A. a chest massage
    B. a hot drink
    C. artificial respiration
    D. an application of cold compresses

33. The LEAST important information to be given to a newly appointed trackman is

    A. a set of train schedules
    B. the name of the foreman to whom he is assigned
    C. a book of safety instructions
    D. his scheduled working hours

34. Trackmen often work in large gangs *mainly* because

    A. fewer foremen are required
    B. it helps morale
    C. many trades are involved
    D. the work is heavy

35. The BEST course for a newly appointed trackman to follow is to

    A. work fast to make a good first impression
    B. show interest in the work
    C. make the foreman repeat every instruction for safety
    D. be on the lookout for chances to avoid unpleasant work assignments

36. When you are working in a large gang, it is MOST important that you

    A. do exactly the same amount of work as the others
    B. check the work of men near you
    C. do your particular assigned job properly
    D. help any man that you think needs help

37. The transit authority does NOT operate any subway in

    A. the Bronx   B. Queens   C. Brooklyn   D. Staten Island

38. Rubber mats are frequently used by workers for protection against 38.____

   A. moving machinery B. fire
   C. electric shock D. falling objects

39. A steel rail exposed to the weather will expand if there is an *increase* in 39.____

   A. temperature B. humidity
   C. air pressure D. wind velocity

40. Creosote used on railroad ties is *primarily* a 40.____

   A. paint B. filler
   C. reinforcement D. preservative

41. A bag of cement will harden if it gets 41.____

   A. old   B. wet   C. hot   D. very cold

42. There are NO signs in the subway which forbid passengers to 42.____

   A. cross tracks B. smoke
   C. talk to employees D. spit

43. A 39-foot length of running rail weighing 100 lbs. per yard has a total weight of _____ lbs. 43.____

   A. 390   B. 780   C. 1,300   D. 3,900

44. The pay of a trackman for a 40-hour week at $9.195 an hour is 44.____

   A. $367.80   B. 369.30   C. 388.80   D. 394.80

45. The number of counties in New York City is 45.____

   A. 3   B. 4   C. 5   D. 6

KEY (CORRECT ANSWERS)

1. B	11. B	21. B	31. D	41. B
2. C	12. D	22. C	32. C	42. C
3. D	13. D	23. C	33. A	43. C
4. B	14. A	24. B	34. D	44. A
5. D	15. B	25. A	35. B	45. C
6. C	16. D	26. A	36. C	
7. A	17. D	27. B	37. D	
8. C	18. A	28. D	38. C	
9. C	19. A	29. C	39. A	
10. D	20. A	30. B	40. D	

TEST 2

DIRECTIONS: Each question or incomplete statement is followed by several suggested answers or completions. Select the one that BEST answers the question or completes the statement. *PRINT THE LETTER OF THE CORRECT ANSWER IN THE SPACE AT THE RIGHT.*

1. A trackman should observe and report to his superior if he notices

    A. passengers crowding into trains
    B. trains running behind schedule
    C. track tools in defective condition
    D. some newspapers on the track

    1.___

2. *Before* using a portable electric drill, a trackman should make sure

    A. the cord is in good condition
    B. it has not been used by anyone else
    C. the handle is not painted
    D. it has just been overhauled

    2.___

3. The LEAST likely result of a severe electric shock is

    A. bleeding
    B. stoppage of breathing
    C. a burn
    D. unconsciousness

    3.___

4. If a trackman working with his foreman near a subway station notices a large puddle of oil on the platform, the trackman should FIRST

    A. clean up the oil
    B. assume that the station porter will take care of it
    C. call it to the attention of his foreman
    D. locate the source of the oil

    4.___

5. The official rules restrict the use of transit system telephones to official business. This means that a trackman should NOT use such telephones to call

    A. his superior for instructions
    B. for an ambulance
    C. for police
    D. his sick child at home

    5.___

6. Trains are LEAST likely to be delayed if a section of track is renewed

    A. in the morning
    B. about noon
    C. in the evening
    D. about midnight

    6.___

7. Sand delivered to a construction job for use in mixing concrete is measured in

    A. bushels   B. bags   C. square feet   D. cubic yards

    7.___

8. A strong foundation is needed under track ties in the subway because the ties

    A. are made of wood
    B. must support a heavy load
    C. break easily
    D. are very heavy

    8.___

2 (#2)

9. A trackman should NOT use a cold chisel with a mushroomed head because the

   A. chisel will not cut
   B. hammer may slip
   C. head may shatter
   D. chisel will bend

10. The MAIN reason for constantly inspecting tracks is to

    A. keep them from getting rusty
    B. eliminate all noises
    C. prevent them from getting dirty
    D. find track defects quickly

11. The designation 10-32 is frequently used to describe a

    A. piece of lumber
    B. machine screw
    C. bolt
    D. drill size

QUESTIONS 12-20.

Questions 12 to 20 inclusive, refer to the paragraph "RAIL JOINTS given below, and to the sketch. Consult the paragraph and sketch in answering these questions.

RAIL JOINTS

The distance between rail ends at all joints must be gauged according to the temperature at which the rails are laid. Metal shims mult be used to space the rail ends at the J^s"d must be removed as soon as the joint bar bolts are tightened and the jail securely anchored. The joint bar bolts are to be applied with their heads alternately inside and outside of the rail ^pring washers for bolts are required at all rail joints. The heads of the bolts must be tight against the joint bar before tightening the nuts, and the nuts must be screwed up tight with an approved track wrench. All joint bars and the parts of the rails covered by them must be care fully painted with an approved oxidation inhibitor.

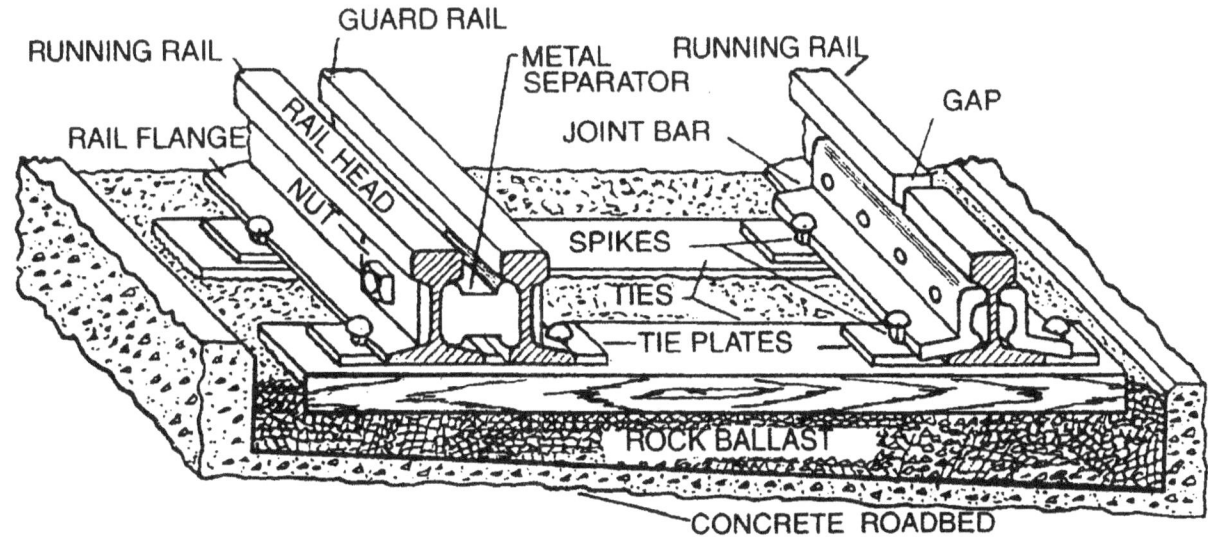

12. Shims must be inserted

    A. if the rails are tightened
    B. when the rails are laid
    C. after the joints are painted
    D. after the bolts are tightened

13. Spring washers are used to

    A. prevent the nuts from loosening
    B. absorb the shock of passing trains
    C. keep the joint bars in place
    D. prevent the gap from closing

14. The number of bolt heads on the inside of a joint is

    A. 1   B. 2   C. 3   D. 4

15. The heads of bolts should be tight against the

    A. huts   B. rails
    C. joint bars   D. spring washers

16. Oxidation inhibitors are used to prevent

    A. leaks   B. rust   C. vibration   D. dampness

17. The track is securely anchored when the rails are spiked to the ties and the

    A. ballast is firmly in place
    B. ties are resting on the roadbed
    C. shims have been removed
    D. joint bars are bolted tightly

18. The distance to be left between rail ends at joints depends on the

    A. temperature   B. shims
    C. number of bolts   D. joint bars

19. The proper order of assembly at the rail joint would be

    A. spikes, rails, joint bars   B. joint bars, rails, spikes
    C. spikes, joint bars, rails   D. rails, joint bars, spikes

20. Shims are used in spacing

    A. joint bars   B. rail ends
    C. bolts   D. spring washers

21. The *greatest* wear on the side of the rail head will be on tracks which are

    A. curved   B. straight
    C. at stations   D. on steep grades

22. The use of intoxicating liquor by employees while on duty is strictly prohibited by the rules of the transit authority *mainly* because the use of such liquor

    A. is expensive
    B. is immoral
    C. adversely affects their judgment
    D. causes a high rate of absenteeism

23. For protection against objects falling from overhead, workers frequently wear   23._____

    A. hard helmets   B. work gloves
    C. safety shoes   D. heavy clothing

24. A *good* fireproof material is   24._____

    A. asbestos   B. canvas   C. wool   D. cotton

25. Pneumatic drills are operated by   25._____

    A. compressed air   B. water pressure
    C. oil pressure   D. steam

26. A policeman should be called if two passengers arguing on a platform   26._____

    A. argue loudly
    B. refuse to enter their train
    C. resort to force
    D. leave the station

27. A trackman frequently missing from his assigned work area will be   27._____

    A. transferred   B. excused
    C. re-instructed   D. disciplined

QUESTIONS 28-45.

Questions 28 to 45 inclusive, refer to the sketch of a portion of subway track and the illustrations of tools shown below. Refer to the sketch when answering these questions.

5 (#2)

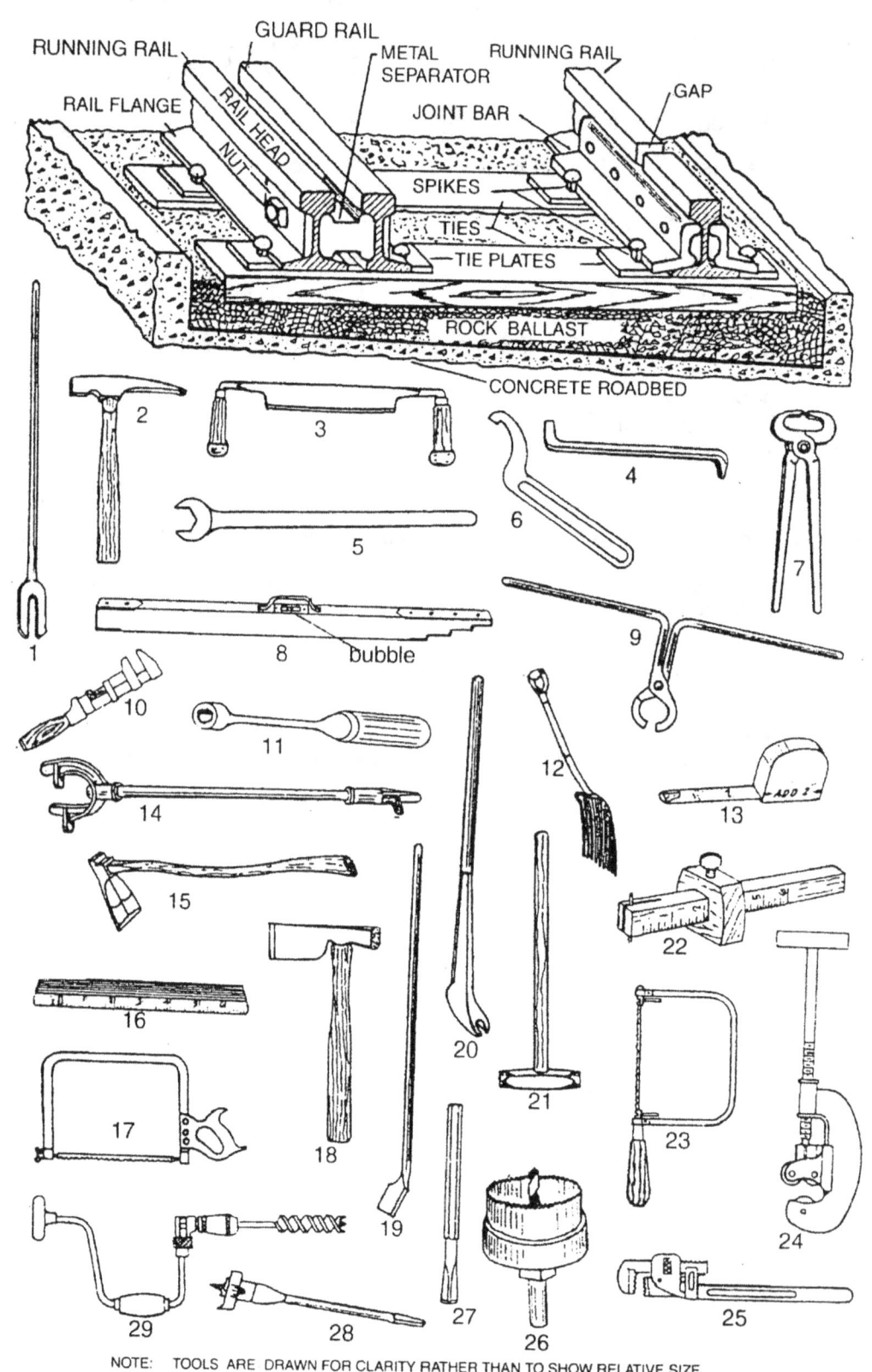

NOTE: TOOLS ARE DRAWN FOR CLARITY RATHER THAN TO SHOW RELATIVE SIZE

28. Rock ballast should be, spread with No.

    A. 19   B. 12   C. 9   D. 1

28.____

6 (#2)

29. The tool for driving rail spikes is No. 29._____
    A. 2   B. 15   C. 18   D. 21

30. The tool for pulling out rail spikes is No. 30._____
    A. 2   B. 7   C. 9   D. 20

31. The tool to be used by two men is carrying a rail is No. 31._____
    A. 20   B. 9   C. 8   D. 7

32. Tamping or forcing rock ballast under a tie is done with No. 32._____
    A. 2   B. 4
    C. 19   D. 27

33. A tool used on the flange for turning over the rail is No. 33._____
    A. 1   B. 5   C. 7   D. 19

34. A difference in level of the two rails of a track is *best* checked with No. 34._____
    A. 8   B. 13   C. 16   D. 22

35. Nuts on track rails are *best* tightened with No. 35._____
    A. 5   B. 6   C. 10   D. 25

36. The standard fixed gauge for spacing the two running rails is No. 36._____
    A. 22   B. 16   C. 14   D. 13

37. A length of rail can be cut by hand using No. 37._____
    A. 15   B. 17   C. 23   D. 24

38. An adze is illustrated by No. 38._____
    A. 2   B. 3   C. 15   D. 18

39. Standard size holes for bolts are *best* drilled through wooden ties by using No. 39._____
    A. 26   B. 27
    C. 28   D. 29

40. The separator between the guard rail and running rail is *most likely* 40._____
    A. aluminum   B. steel   C. silver   D. tin

41. A hole could be drilled in concrete using Nos. 41._____
    A. 2 and 26   B. 27 and 2
    C. 18 and 4   D. 26 and 21

42. A spanner wrench is illustrated by No. 42._____
    A. 3   B. 4   C. 6   D. 11

43. Two tools which are *primarily* for use on iron pipe are Nos.

    A. 10 and 11   B. 7 and 26
    C. 4 and 6   D. 24 and 25

44. As shown by the ballast, one running rail is higher than the other because the track is *probably*

    A. on a down-grade   B. on an up-grad
    C. on a curve   D. at a station

45. The spacing between the running rail and guard rail is *necessary* to allow for

    A. the separator
    B. tightening the nut
    C. wheel flanges
    D. correct running rail spacing

KEY (CORRECT ANSWERS)

1. C	11. B	21. A	31. B	41. B
2. A	12. B	22. C	32. C	42. C
3. A	13. A	23. A	33. A	43. D
4. C	14. B	24. A	34. A	44. C
5. D	15. C	25. A	35. A	45. C
6. D	16. B	26. C	36. C	
7. D	17. A	27. D	37. B	
8. B	18. A	28. B	38. C	
9. C	19. D	29. D	39. D	
10. D	20. B	30. D	40. B	

EXAMINATION SECTION
TEST 1

DIRECTIONS: Each question or incomplete statement is followed by several suggested answers or completions. Select the one that BEST answers the question or completes the statement. *PRINT THE LETTER OF THE CORRECT ANSWER IN THE SPACE AT THE RIGHT.*

1. On curves, an extra rail is usually bolted to the lower rail.
   This extra rail is called a

   A. derail B. guard rail C. power rail D. signal rail

2. "Lay-up" tracks are *primarily* used for

   A. express trains
   B. special trains
   C. train storage
   D. local trains

3. In storage yards, the dead end of the track is fitted with a bumping block.
   The MAIN reason for using this bumping block is to

   A. prevent a stopped train from rolling
   B. prevent collision between two trains
   C. permit trains to be parked without strain on the brakes
   D. stop a train that is out of control

4. Pneumatic concrete breakers are operated by

   A. water pressure
   B. oil pressure
   C. acetylene
   D. compressed air

5. "Rail braces" are used wherever it is necessary to brace a rail sideways.
   As a trackman you should expect to find such rail braces

   A. at steep grades
   B. at stations
   C. on straight track
   D. on curves

6. Steel "tie plates" are used between the bottom of track rails and the top of wooden ties.
   The purpose of such tie plates is to keep the rails from

   A. cutting into the ties
   B. moving the ties
   C. splitting the ties
   D. bending the ties

7. "Anti-creepers" are metal clamps that are affixed to the bottom of track rails to reduce the rail's tendency to slide in the direction of train traffic.
   As a trackman, you should expect to find such anti-creepers

   A. midway between ties
   B. at track joints
   C. tight against the ties
   D. tight against insulated joints

8. When driving a cut spike through a small tie plate into a tie, a trackman should expect that the *greatest* damage would result from hitting the

   A. tie plate B. tie C. rail D. spike

9. A blue light along the tracks indicates the location of an emergency power cut-off and

   A. a signal box
   B. a telephone
   C. an insulated joint
   D. emergency tools

10. The advantage of using cut spikes instead of screw spikes is that cut spikes

    A. damage the rails less
    B. damage the ties less
    C. are much stronger
    D. can be installed more quickly

QUESTIONS 11-19.

Questions 11-19 are based on the paragraph "Flagging Rules." In answering these questions refer to this paragraph.

Flagging Rules

When a track gang is going to work under flagging protection at a given location, the Desk Trainmaster of the division must be notified. Work on trainways must not be performed on operating tracks between 6:00 AM and 9:00 AM, or between 4:00 PM and 7:00 PM. A flagman must be selected from the list of flagmen qualified as such by the Assistant General Superintendent. No person acting as a flagman may be assigned any duties other than those of a flagman. For underground flagging signals, lighted lanterns must be used. Out of doors, flags at least 23" x 29" in dimensions, must be used between sunrise and sunset. Moving a red light across the track is the prescribed stop signal under normal flagging conditions. Moving a white light up and down means proceed slowly. A red light must never be used to give a proceed signal. Moving a yellow light up and down is a signal to a motorman to proceed very slowly. On the track to be worked on, two yellow lights must be displayed at a point not less than 500 feet, nor more than 700 feet, in approach to the flagman's station. On any track where caution lights are displayed, one green light must be displayed a safe distance beyond the farthest point of work. Caution lights must be displayed on the right hand side of the track.

11. Before starting work on a track, the transit official who should be notified is the

    A. General Superintendent
    B. Assistant General Superintendent
    C. Desk Trainmaster
    D. Yardmaster

12. It is permissible to start work on an operating track at

    A. 8 AM   B. 11 AM   C. 4 PM   D. 6 PM

13. A flagman for a track gang MUST be selected from

    A. men on light duty
    B. disabled men
    C. a list of qualified men
    D. senior trackmen

14. The flagman who is protecting a working gang of trackmen

    A. should lend a hand when needed in heavy lifting
    B. should clean up the track area while awaiting trains
    C. must not be assigned to other duties
    D. can collect scrap iron while awaiting trains

15. The prescribed "stop" signal is given by moving a

   A. red light up and down
   B. green light up and down
   C. red light across the tracks
   D. green light across the tracks

16. The normal "proceed slowly" signal is given by moving a

   A. red light up and down
   B. white light up and down
   C. yellow light across the tracks
   D. green light across the tracks

17. Of the following, an *acceptable* distance between a work area and the yellow lights is _____ feet.

   A. 300   B. 600   C. 800   D. 1000

18. A green light should be displayed

   A. at the flagman's location
   B. directly in front of the work area
   C. at the midpoint of the work area
   D. a safe distance beyond the work area

19. Caution lights should be displayed

   A. on the left hand side of the track
   B. on the right hand side of the track
   C. between the tracks
   D. next to the third rail

20. To prevent a saw blade from binding in a cut slot, the teeth of the saw are *usually*

   A. set sideways alternately
   B. made of a thickness greater than the rest of the blade
   C. bent forward in the cutting direction
   D. made with alternating long and short teeth

21. Safe practice dictates that when using a portable electric drill a trackman should

   A. ground the frame
   B. run it at a slow speed
   C. connect a bank of lamps across the power leads
   D. connect a lamp in series with the positive lead

22. If a drill breaks in a steel plate, the *most likely* cause of this breakage is that the

   A. drill speed is too slow
   B. drill hits a hard spot in the steel
   C. steel is too soft
   D. drill feed is excessive

4 (#1)

23. To cut the ends of a number of lengths of wood at an angle of 45 degrees, it would be BEST to use a

   A. protractor B. triangle C. miter-box D. wooden rule

24. The MOST important reason for keeping a cold chisel free from oil or grease is to

   A. prevent a fire hazard when the tool is heated
   B. avoid oil splattering from the hammer blows
   C. prevent the hammer from glancing off the chisel head
   D. make it cut better

25. If a section of track has a pitch of 1/8-inch per foot the total rise in 250 feet of track will be *most nearly* _____ inches.

   A. 3 B. 20 C. 31 D. 2000

26. The MOST important reason for maintaining CORRECT spacing between track ties is to

   A. use fewer joints   B. use fewer ties
   C. make trackwalking safer   D. provide good track support

27. To quickly shut off the third rail power on any track, emergency switch boxes are provided along the tracks. One *logical* reason for operating the emergency box would be to

   A. prevent a train from hitting a trackwalker
   B. shut off power in case of a fire on the track
   C. switch power to alternate tracks
   D. permit routine cleaning of the tracks

28. Assume that a trackman earns $24,000 a year. If twenty per cent of his pay is deducted for taxes and social security, his weekly take home pay will be *most nearly*

   A. $326 B. $370 C. $462 D. $19,200

29. The purpose of using lock washers on bolts which fasten splice plates in place is to

   A. keep the plates from turning
   B. prevent the nuts from loosening
   C. make removal of the nuts easier
   D. avoid stripping the threads

QUESTIONS 30-33.

Questions 30-33 refer to the drawing "Holes in Track Tie."

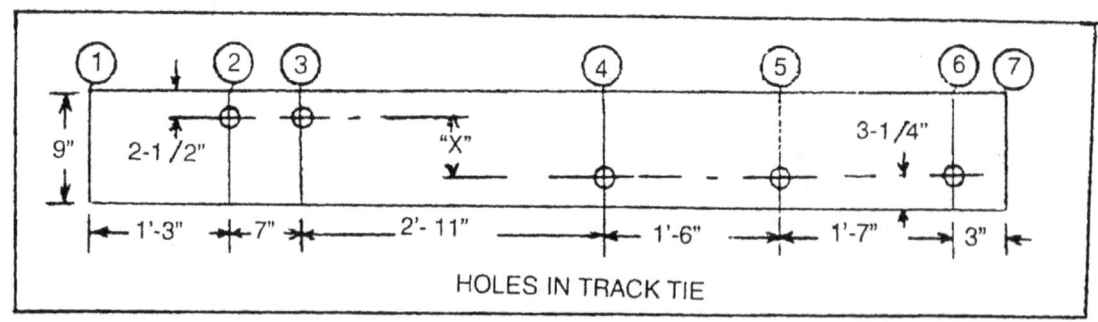

HOLES IN TRACK TIE

30. The distance from 1 to 4 is 30._____

   A. 4'-5"   B. 4'-7"   C. 4'-9"   D. 4'-11"

31. The distance from 2 to 6 is 31._____

   A. 5'-0"   B. 5'-1"   C. 6'-0"   D. 6'-7"

32. The entire length of the tie, from 1 to 7 is 32._____

   A. 7'-10"   B. 8'-1"   C. 8'-4"   D. 8'-7"

33. The distance "X" between the lines of holes is 33._____

   A. 2 1/2"   B. 2-3/4"   C. 3"   D. 3 1/4"

34. Extending the handle of a track wrench by using a piece of pipe to *increase* leverage when tightening a large nut is considered BAD practice because the 34._____

   A. pipe may break
   B. pipe may be burred
   C. threads may be stripped
   D. wrench may be damaged

35. The MOST important reason for dipping a chisel into cold water when it is being ground is to 35._____

   A. preserve the temper of the chisel
   B. keep the chisel clean
   C. provide lubrication for the grinding
   D. reduce the wear on the grinding wheel

36. The distance required for a train to make a full stop depends MOST on the 36._____

   A. train speed   B. wheel condition
   C. type of car coupling   D. width of the wheels

37. Gloves should be used when handling 37._____

   A. wooden rules   B. lanterns
   C. creosoted ties D. all small tools

38. It is recommended that shoes which have a sponge rubber sole should NOT be worn by trackmen on the job because such a sole 38._____

   A. is not waterproof
   B. wears out too quickly
   C. does not keep the feet warm enough
   D. is easily punctured by steel objects

39. The MAIN purpose of the stone ballast under some tracks is to 39._____

   A. keep proper tie spacing
   B. cushion the ties
   C. maintain proper line
   D. provide electrical insulation

40. The rules of the transit authority require a trackman to give notice of his intention to be absent from work several hours before he is scheduled to report for duty.
The MAIN reason for having this rule is that

    A. the track gang can be reassigned to a different job
    B. a new man can be trained to take this man's place
    C. it permits time for a doctor to be sent to the trackman's home
    D. it allows time for assigning a substitute

KEY (CORRECT ANSWERS)

1. B	11. C	21. A	31. D
2. C	12. B	22. D	32. B
3. D	13. C	23. C	33. D
4. D	14. C	24. C	34. C
5. D	15. C	25. C	35. A
6. A	16. B	26. D	36. A
7. C	17. B	27. B	37. C
8. C	18. D	28. B	38. D
9. B	19. B	29. B	39. B
10. D	20. A	30. C	40. D

TEST 2

DIRECTIONS: Each question or incomplete statement is followed by several suggested answers or completions. Select the one that BEST answers the question or completes the statement. *PRINT THE LETTER OF THE CORRECT ANSWER IN THE SPACE AT THE RIGHT.*

QUESTIONS 1-18.

Questions 1-18 on the following page refer to the numbered tools shown below. Refer to these tools when answering those questions.

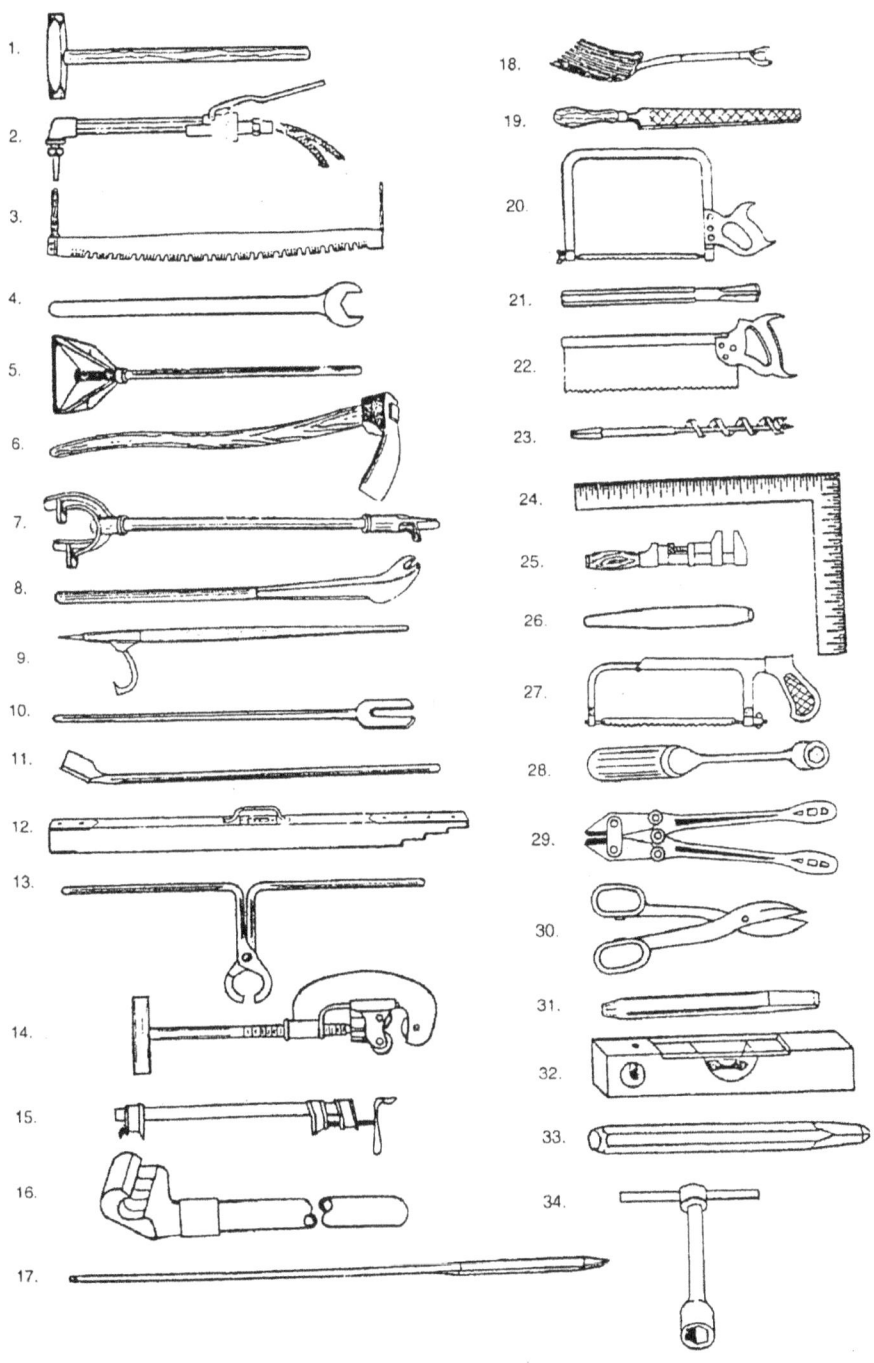

2 (#2)

1. To cut holes in concrete for lead anchors, a trackman should use tool no.
   A. 21   B. 26   C. 31   D. 33

2. To smooth off the burrs from the end of a track rail, a trackman should use tool no.
   A. 2   B. 19   C. 27   D. 31

3. To cut a 2" x 1/4" steel bar into two pieces, a trackman should use tool no.
   A. 3   B. 14   C. 27   D. 30

4. To drill a 3/4" dia. hole through a wood plank, a trackman should use tool no.
   A. 2   B. 15   C. 21   D. 23

5. To cut an 8" x 10" wooden tie into four pieces, a trackman should use tool no.
   A. 3   B. 20   C. 22   D. 27

6. To cut a 1/4" diameter multi-stranded steel cable, a trackman should use tool no.
   A. 14   B. 22   C. 29   D. 30

7. To drive rail spikes, a trackman should use tool no.
   A. 1   B. 5   C. 6   D. 8

8. To carry a rail, trackmen should use tool no.
   A. 7   B. 8   C. 11   D. 13

9. To tighten the nuts on track bolts, a trackman should use tool no.
   A. 4   B. 16   C. 25   D. 34

10. To line-up the holes when installing fish plates, a trackman should use tool no.
    A. 10   B. 17   C. 26   D. 33

11. To cut 1-inch diameter pipe separators, a trackman should use tool no.
    A. 3   B. 14   C. 22   D. 30

12. To spread rock ballast, a trackman should use tool no.
    A. 5   B. 8   C. 17   D. 18

13. To check the gauge between rails, a trackman should use tool no.
    A. 7   B. 12   C. 15   D. 32

14. To turn over a rail, trackmen should use tool no.
    A. 8   B. 9   C. 10   D. 11

15. To check the squareness of the end of a protection board, a trackman should use tool no.
    A. 12   B. 15   C. 24   D. 32

16. To pull out cut spikes, a trackman should use tool no.   16.____

   A. 6   B. 8   C. 10   D. 17

17. To dap a tie, a trackman should use tool no.   17.____

   A. 2   B. 6   C. 16   D. 19

18. To cut frozen track bolts, a trackman should use tool no.   18.____

   A. 1   B. 2   C. 14   D. 33

19. The sum of 3-1/16", 4 1/4", 2-5/8" and 5-7/16" is   19.____

   A. 15-3/16"   B. 15 1/4"   C. 15-3/8"   D. 15 1/2"

20. A concrete foundation is frequently poured beneath track ties *mainly* in order to   20.____

   A. keep the ties dry
   B. support a heavy load
   C. avoid tie replacement
   D. make tie renewal easier

21. A cold chisel with a head that is badly beaten out of shape should NOT be used *mainly* because it   21.____

   A. may be unsafe to use
   B. will cut poorly
   C. may soon bend
   D. may be impossible to dress

22. Artificial respiration should be given immediately to a man who has suffered an electric shock and is   22.____

   A. unconscious and breathing heavily
   B. unconscious and not breathing
   C. conscious and very hot
   D. conscious and very cold

23. The MAIN reason why a trackman should have a general knowledge of all the tools and equipment assigned to his gang is that each trackman   23.____

   A. uses all of the tools every day
   B. must know how to repair each tool
   C. may someday have to use each item
   D. is responsible for teaching new men how to use each item

24. When grinding a weld smooth, it is MOST important to avoid   24.____

   A. grinding too slowly
   B. overheating the surrounding metal
   C. grinding too much of the weld away
   D. grinding after the weld has cooled off

25. The MAIN reason why the transit authority has trackmen *constantly* inspecting the tracks is to   25.____

   A. keep the men busy
   B. find track defects as soon as possible
   C. have men available in an emergency
   D. instill confidence in passengers

26. A slight coating of rust on small tools is BEST removed by

    A. rubbing with a dry cloth
    B. scraping with a sharp knife
    C. wiping with a slight coat of vaseline
    D. rubbing with kerosene and fine steel wool

27. The rules of the transit authority require a trackman who discovers a fire in the subway to telephone the trainmaster, giving his name, badge number and the location of the fire. The MAIN reason for requiring the trackman to give his name and badge number is that this

    A. avoids false alarms
    B. enables the trackman to be rewarded
    C. helps in the subsequent investigation of the fire
    D. helps determine whether the trackman started the fire

28. If a trackman gets $10.40 per hour and time and one-half for working over 40 hours, his gross salary for a week in which he worked 44 hours should be

    A. $457.60   B. $478.40   C. $499.20   D. $514.80

QUESTIONS 29-37.

Questions 29-37 refer to the pile of wood ties shown below. Refer to this sketch when answering these questions.

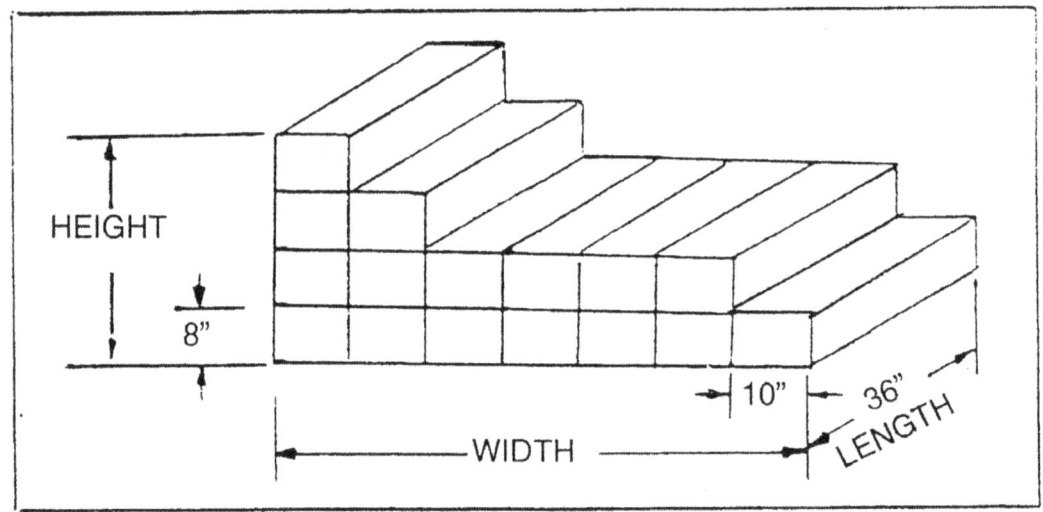

29. The *total* number of ties shown is

    A. 18   B. 17   C. 16   D. 15

30. The MAXIMUM height of the pile is

    A. 40"   B. 32"   C. 24"   D. 8"

31. The WIDTH of the pile is

    A. 3'-0"   B. 5'-10"   C. 6'-2"   D. 7'-0"

5 (#2)

32. The LOWEST height of any part of the pile is 32._____
    A. 32"   B. 16"   C. 10"   D. 8"

33. The pile is greater in 33._____
    A. height than in width
    B. height than in length
    C. length than in width
    D. length than in height

34. The total number of ties which do NOT rest directly on the ground is 34._____
    A. 10   B. 9   C. 8   D. 7

35. If all the ties shown are rearranged into a solid pile with an even height of 4 layers high, then the new pile will have a width of _____ ties. 35._____
    A. 3   B. 4   C. 5   D. 6

36. The size of each tie is 36._____
    A. 8" x 8" x 3'-0"
    B. 8" x 18" x 2'-6"
    C. 8" x 10" x 3'-0"
    D. 10" x 10" x 2'-6"

37. If the material of the ties weighs 1/40 of a pound per cubic inch, the weight of a tie is _____ pounds. 37._____
    A. 58   B. 66   C. 72   D. 78

38. When cutting a steel rod with a hacksaw, it is GOOD practice to 38._____
    A. use very short, rapid strokes
    B. use heavy pressure on both the forward and return strokes
    C. slow the speed of cutting when the piece is almost cut through
    D. increase the speed of cutting when the piece is almost cut through

39. If a one inch diameter hole is to be made in the web of a steel rail, the BEST method to use is 39._____
    A. punching
    B. reaming
    C. drilling
    D. cutting with a torch

40. A small gap is provided between rail lengths at track joints *mainly* for 40._____
    A. expansion
    B. ease in replacing rail
    C. vibration
    D. wear

KEY (CORRECT ANSWERS)

1. A	11. B	21. A	31. B
2. B	12. D	22. B	32. D
3. C	13. A	23. C	33. D
4. D	14. C	24. C	34. B
5. A	15. C	25. B	35. B
6. C	16. B	26. D	36. C
7. A	17. B	27. C	37. C
8. D	18. B	28. B	38. C
9. A	19. C	29. C	39. C
10. C	20. B	30. B	40. A

EXAMINATION SECTION
TEST 1

DIRECTIONS: Each question or incomplete statement is followed by several suggested answers or completions. Select the one that BEST answers the question or completes the statement. *PRINT THE LETTER OF THE CORRECT ANSWER IN THE SPACE AT THE RIGHT.*

QUESTIONS 1-10.
Questions 1-10 are based on the sketch below which shows a small section of subway track.

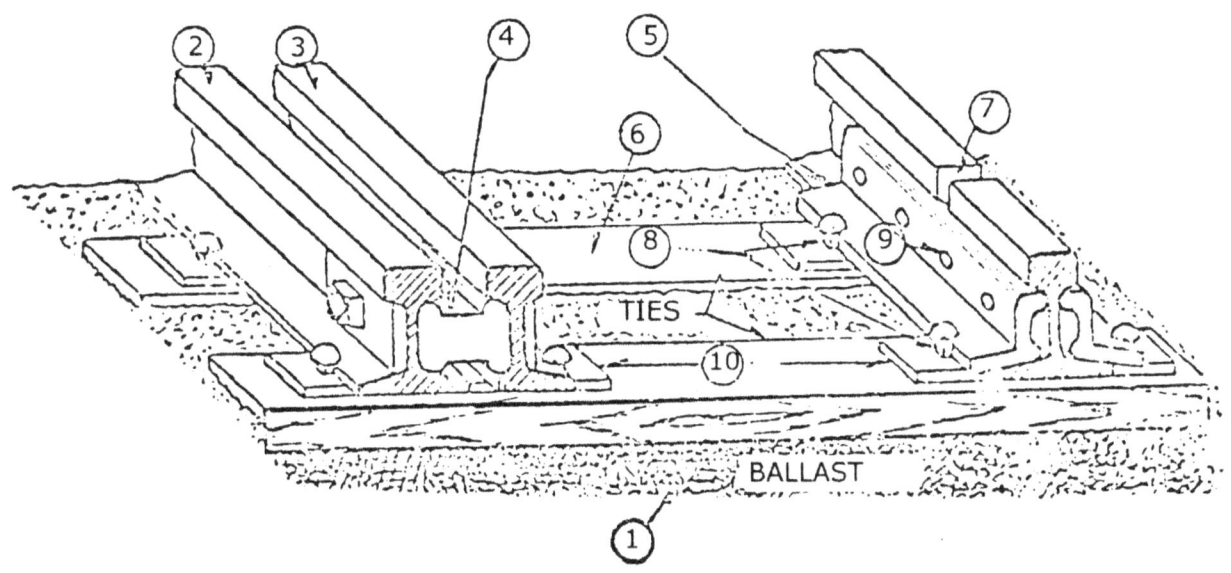

1. Ballast 1 is made of

   A. concrete   B. cinders   C. gravel   D. steel

   1.____

2. Rail 2 is a _____ rail.

   A. third   B. running   C. guard   D. emergency

   2.____

3. Rail 3 is a _____ rail.

   A. third   B. running   C. guard   D. emergency

   3.____

4. Track part 4 is a

   A. divider   B. separator   C. connector   D. filler

   4.____

5. Track part 5 is a

   A. connector   B. fish plate   C. tie plate   D. carryover plate

   5.____

6. Tie 6 is made of

   A. wood   B. steel   C. concrete   D. rubber

   6.____

7. Gap 7 is provided for

   A. vibration   B. wear   C. settlement   D. expansion

   7.____

2 (#1)

8. Track part 8 is a

   A. cut spike B. screw spike C. rivet D. bolt

9. Bolt 9 is a

   A. tie bolt B. expansion bolt
   C. track bolt D. carriage bolt

10. Track part 10 is a _____ plate.

    A. fish B. expansion C. tie D. track

11. The MOST dangerous track condition for a train is a

    A. shiny rail B. slightly worn rail
    C. wet tie D. broken rail

12. If a section of ballast 6'-0" wide, 8'-0" long, and 2'-6" deep is excavated, the amount of ballast removed is _____ cu. feet.

    A. 96 B. 104 C. 120 D. 144

13. The wall area behind the metal ladders that are permanently fastened into the subway wall is often painted yellow in order to

    A. prevent accumulation of dirt
    B. make the ladders easily visible
    C. prevent rusting of the fastenings
    D. reduce reflection from the wall

14. The weight per foot of a length of square-bar 4" x 4" in cross section, as compared with one 2" x 2" in cross section is _____ as much.

    A. twice B. 2 1/2 times C. 3 times D. 4 times

15. An order for 360 feet of 2" x 8" lumber is shipped in 20-foot lengths. The MAXIMUM number of 9-foot pieces that can be cut from this shipment is

    A. 54 B. 40 C. 36 D. 18

16. When track work is being done on the elevated structure, canvas spreads are suspended under the working area *mainly* to

    A. reduce noise B. discourage crowds
    C. protect the structure D. protect pedestrians

17. The MOST important reason for maintaining correct spacing between track ties is to

    A. provide good track support B. use fewer ties
    C. make trackwalking safe D. use fewer joints

18. The MAIN reason employees are forbidden to hang flags or lights of any description on subway signals is to avoid

    A. fire hazard B. damage to signal equipment
    C. confusing the motormen D. loss of such articles

19. The distance covered in three minutes by a subway train traveling at 30 mph is 19.____

    A. 3 miles B. 2 miles C. 1 1/2 miles D. 1 mile

20. The advantage of track cut spikes over track screw spikes is that cut spikes 20.____

    A. damage the rails less
    B. damage the ties less
    C. are much stronger
    D. can be installed more quickly

21. A crate contains 3 pieces of equipment weighing 73, 84, and 47 pounds respectively. The 21.____
    empty crate weighs 16 pounds. If the crate is lifted by 4 trackmen, each trackman lifting
    one corner of the crate, the average number of pounds lifted by each of the trackmen is

    A. 68 B. 61 C. 55 D. 51

22. The distance required for a train to make a full stop depends MOST on the 22.____

    A. width of the wheels   B. type of car coupling
    C. condition of the wheels   D. train speed

23. Gloves should be used when handling 23.____

    A. all small tools   B. creosoted ties
    C. lanterns   D. wooden rules

QUESTIONS 24-27.
Questions 24-27 are based on the information contained in the safety rules given below. In
answering these questions refer to these rules.

Safety Rules for Employees Working on Tracks

Always carry a hand lantern whenever walking a track and walk opposite to the direction of traffic on that particular track, if possible.

At all times when walking track, take note of and be prepared to use the spaces available for safety. Be careful to avoid those positions where clearance is insufficient.

Employees are particularly cautioned with respect to sections of track on which regular operation of passenger trains may at times be abandoned and which are used as lay-up tracks. Such tracks are likely to be used at irregular times by special trains such as work trains, lay-up trains, etc. At no time can any section of track be assumed to be definitely out of service and employees myst observe, when on or near tracks, the usual precautions regardless of any assumption as to operating schedules.

24. An employee walking a section of track should walk 24.____

    A. to the left of the tracks
    B. to the right of the tracks
    C. opposite to the direction of traffic
    D. in the direction of traffic

25. One precaution an employee should ALWAYS take when walking along the tracks is to

    A. note nearby safety spaces
    B. wave his lantern constantly when walking track
    C. place a red lantern behind him when walking track
    D. have power turned off on those tracks on which he is walking

26. On sections of track NOT used for regular passenger trains, an employee should

    A. disregard the usual precautions
    B. walk in the direction of traffic
    C. assume that no trains will be operating
    D. follow the rules governing tracks in passenger train operation

27. Lay-up tracks are NOT likely to be used by

    A. special trains
    B. trains carrying passengers
    C. work trains
    D. lay-up trains

28. In subway stations, a fixed narrow wooden strip is generally fastened to the edge of the concrete platforms. The MAIN reason for this practice is to avoid

    A. damage to a swaying train
    B. slipping by passengers leaving trains
    C. large gaps between cars and platforms
    D. a sharp edge on the edge of a platform

29. An employee is NOT permitted to give a passenger a description of any lost article which the employee has found and turned in because

    A. employees are not permitted to hold long conversations with passengers
    B. this might aid the passenger in claiming property not belonging to him
    C. this would delay the employee in his work
    D. the employee may make a mistake in the description

30. Much of the replacement of track rails is done at night *mainly* because

    A. trains can be switched to single track operation only at night
    B. trains make better time at night
    C. many men prefer night work
    D. fewer trains run at night

31. Because of the danger of the third rail, it would be BEST for trackmen to use work pails made of

    A. iron   B. steel   C. fiber   D. brass

32. The measurements of a poured concrete track foundation shows that 54 cubic feet of concrete has been placed. If payment to the transit-mix company for this concrete is to be on the basis of cubic yards, the 54 cubic feet must be

    A. multiplied by 27
    B. divided by 27
    C. multiplied by 3
    D. divided by 3

33. A strong foundation is needed under track ties because the ties   33.____

    A. are made of wood
    B. must support a heavy load
    C. break easily
    D. are very heavy

34. The metal which is *most likely* to crack when struck a heavy blow is   34.____

    A. malleable iron   B. forged steel
    C. cast iron   D. wrought iron

35. The MOST important reason for wearing strong heavy shoes when working on subway   35.____
    track is to

    A. avoid colds   B. obtain longer wear
    C. reduce fatigue   D. avoid injury

36. Before stepping onto a subway track, a trackman should   36.____

    A. find out whether power is on
    B. turn his lantern off
    C. look up and down the track
    D. notify the foreman

37. When trackmen are working on track which is in service, a whistle should be used to indi-   37.____
    cate that

    A. the power is on
    B. the power is off
    C. a train is approaching
    D. the signal system is to be disconnected

38. Pneumatic hammers are operated by   38.____

    A. compressed air   B. acetylene
    C. water pressure   D. oil pressure

39. The sum of 7'-2 3/4", 0'-2 7/8", 3'-0", 4'-6 3/8" and 1'-9 1/4" is   39.____

    A. 16'-8 1/4"   B. 16'-8 3/4"   C. 16'-9 1/4"   D. 16'-9 3/

40. Tools which are damaged should   40.____

    A. be used *only* for unimportant work
    B. be used if repairing them would be expensive
    C. never be used because a trackman may be held responsible for the damage
    D. not be used because personal injury may result

KEY (CORRECT ANSWERS)

1.	C	11.	D	21.	C	31.	C
2.	B	12.	C	22.	D	32.	B
3.	C	13.	B	23.	B	33.	B
4.	B	14.	D	24.	C	34.	C
5.	B	15.	C	25.	A	35.	D
6.	A	16.	D	26.	D	36.	C
7.	D	17.	A	27.	B	37.	C
8.	A	18.	C	28.	A	38.	A
9.	C	19.	C	29.	B	39.	C
10.	C	20.	D	30.	D	40.	D

TEST 2

DIRECTIONS: Each question or incomplete statement is followed by several suggested answers or completions. Select the one that BEST answers the question or completes the statement. *PRINT THE LETTER OF THE CORRECT ANSWER IN THE SPACE AT THE RIGHT.*

QUESTIONS 1-18.
Questions 1-18 refer to the tool shown to the right of each question.

1. A trackman should use this tool to

    A. place concrete
    B. remove ballast
    C. move ties
    D. pick up dirt

1._____

2. A trackman should use this tool to

    A. pull screw spikes
    B. turn rail over
    C. move ties
    D. tighten track bolts

2._____

3. A trackman should use this tool to cut

    A. holes in fish plates
    B. frozen track bolts
    C. long track spikes
    D. the third rail

3._____

4. A trackman should use this tool to

    A. knock off frozen nuts
    B. move rails
    C. drive cut spikes
    D. break up ballast

4._____

5. A trackman should use this tool to

    A. insert cut spikes
    B. drive screw spiKes
    C. tighten track plates
    D. tighten track bolts

5._____

6. A trackman should use this tool to cut

    A. protection boards
    B. long ties
    C. frozen track bolts
    D. rails

6._____

7. A trackman should this tool to

   A. cut ties in two
   B. dap a tie
   C. fit protection board
   D. place ties

7.___

8. A trackman should use this tool to

   A. level ties
   B. level track
   C. space running rails
   D. space the third rail

8.___

9. A trackman should use this tool to

   A. pull cut spikes
   B. move rails
   C. space ties
   D. tighten screw spikes

9.___

10. A trackman should use this tool to

    A. move ties
    B. lift rails
    C. pull track spikes
    D. space rails

10.___

11. A trackman should use this tool to

    A. carry rails
    B. carry ties
    C. move ties
    D. locate the third rail

11.___

12. A trackman should use this tool to

    A. enlarge bolt holes
    B. cut off track bolts
    C. notch rails prior to breaking
    D. smooth rough edges of rails

12.___

13. A trackman should use this tool to

    A. tamp ballast
    B. move rails
    C. drive cut spikes
    D. drive ties into ballast

13.___

14. A trackman should use this tool to cut

    A. rails
    B. pipe
    C. concrete
    D. ties

14._____

15. A trackman should know that this wrench is commonly called a

    A. torque wrench
    B. rachet wrench
    C. off-set wrench
    D. T-wrench

15._____

16. A trackman should use this tool to cut

    A. pipe
    B. sheet metal
    C. nails
    D. wire mesh

16._____

17. A trackman should use this tool on

    A. tangent track
    B. curves
    C. switches
    D. frogs

17._____

18. A trackman should use this tool to

    A. enlarge bolt holes
    B. plug tie holes
    C. line up holes
    D. countersink spikes

18._____

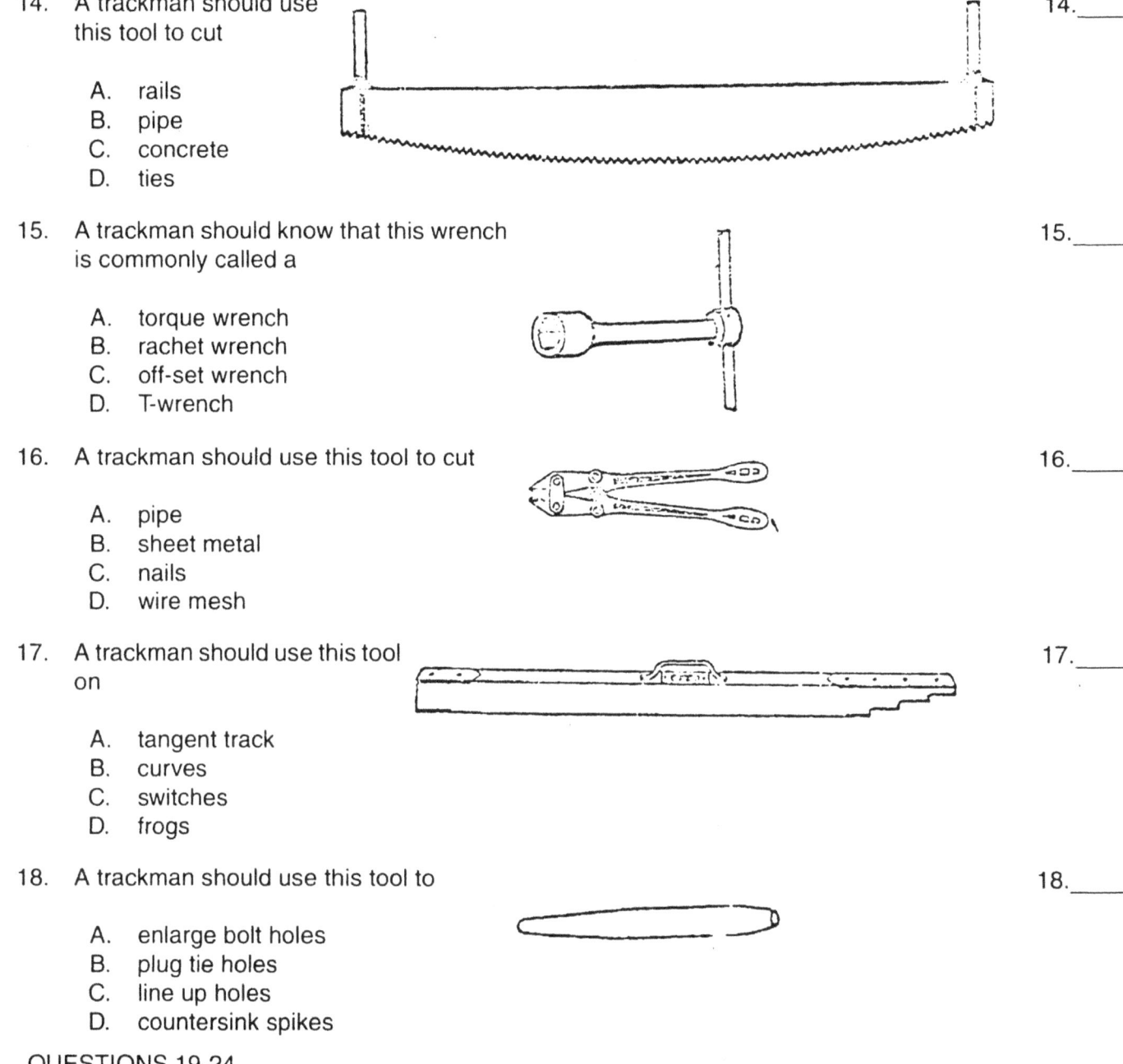

QUESTIONS 19-24.
Questions 19-24 are based on the paragraph "First Aid Instructions".
In answering these questions, refer to this paragraph.

First Aid Instructions

The main purpose of first aid is to put the injured person in the best possible position until medical help arrives. This includes the performance of emergency treatment designed to save a life if a doctor is not immediately available. When an accident happens a crowd usually collects around the victim. If nobody uses his head, the injured person fails to receive the care he needs. You must keep calm and cool at all times and, most important, it is your duty to take charge at an accident. The first thing for you to do is to see, insofar as possible, what is wrong with the injured person. Leave him where he is until the nature and extent of his injury are determined. If he is unconscious he should not be moved except to lay him flat on his back if he is in some other position. Loosen the clothing of any seriously hurt person and make him as comfortable as possible. Medical help should be called as soon as possible. You should remain with the injured person and send someone else to call the doctor. You should try to make sure that the one who calls for a doctor is able to give correct information as to the location of the injured person. In order to help the physician to know what equipment may be needed in each particular case, the person making the call should give the doctor as much information about the injury as possible.

19. If nobody uses his head at the scene of an accident, there is danger that

    A. a large crowd will gather
    B. emergency treatment will be needed
    C. names of witnesses will be missed
    D. the victim will not get the care he needs

20. The FIRST thing you should do at the scene of an accident is to

    A. call a doctor
    B. lay the injured person on his back
    C. find out what is wrong with the injured person
    D. loosen the clothing of the injured person

21. Until the nature and extent of the injuries are determined, you should

    A. move the injured person indoors
    B. let the injured person lie where he is
    C. carefully roll the injured person on his back
    D. give the injured person artificial respiration

22. If the injured person is unconscious, you should

    A. give him artificial respiration
    B. get some hot liquid like coffee into him
    C. lay him flat on his back
    D. move him to a comfortable location

23. If a doctor is to be called, you should

    A. go make this call yourself since you have all the information
    B. go make this call yourself since you are in charge
    C. send someone who knows what happened
    D. send someone who is fast

24. The person calling the doctor should give as much information as he has regarding the injury so that the doctor

    A. can bring the necessary equipment
    B. can decide whether he should come
    C. will know whom to notify
    D. can advise what should be done

25. Subway trains are kept on the track by flanges on the wheels which bear on 25.____

   A. the outside of both rails
   B. both sides of both rails
   C. the inside of both rails
   D. the inside of one rail and the outside of the other

26. Subway track rails rest on ties rather than directly on a concrete bed because the ties 26.____

   A. raise the rail higher
   B. give added strength
   C. give a softer ride
   D. keep the rail dry

27. To quickly shut off the third rail power on any track, emergency switch boxes are provided along the tracks. One *logical* reason for operating the emergency box would be to 27.____

   A. prevent a train from hitting a trackwalker
   B. shut off power in case of a fire on the track
   C. switch power to alternate tracks
   D. signal the motorman in an approaching train

28. When a gang of trackmen is working on a track, one man does nothing else but act as a flagman. 28.____
   This procedure

   A. helps the rest of the gang to work safely
   B. relieves the motorman of responsibility
   C. tends to place too much responsibility on one man
   D. tends to waste time

29. Trackmen often work in large gangs *mainly* because 29.____

   A. fewer foremen are required
   B. it helps morale
   C. many different trades are involved
   D. the work is heavy and covers quite an area

30. One of the two running rails is sometimes installed *higher* than the other. 30.____
   This condition is MOST often found

   A. on curves   B. in stations
   C. in storage yards   D. on grades

31. The BEST first-aid treatment to give a person who has stopped breathing is to 31.____

   A. massage his chest
   B. give him a hot drink
   C. apply artificial respiration
   D. apply cold compresses

32. The MAIN reason why worn track rails are sometimes removed from main lines and reused in train storage yards is that

    A. yard trains are empty and therefore lighter
    B. yards are seldom used
    C. the worn rail is lighter
    D. yard trains travel at lower speeds

33. The proper tool for making a 3/4" diameter hole through a wooden tie is

    A. a reamer
    B. a round chisel
    C. an auger
    D. a countersink

34. A trackman should ordinarily expect that a subway train approaching a sharp curve will

    A. stop
    B. speed up
    C. slow down
    D. continue at the same speed

35. Grease on the track rails is *most likely* to cause

    A. derailment of trains
    B. wheel slippage when trains start or stop
    C. rusting of the rails
    D. rotting of ties

36. Lock washers are used on bolts which fasten splice bars in place in order to

    A. make removal of the nuts easier
    B. avoid stripping the threads
    C. keep the bolts from turning
    D. prevent the nuts from loosening

37. Subway employees are forbidden to cross tracks from one platform to another unless absolutely necessary.
    The MAIN purpose of this rule is to

    A. avoid train delays
    B. prevent confusion
    C. protect the employees
    D. prevent interference with track work

38. The MAIN reason for inspecting tracks *constantly* is to

    A. keep the trackmen busy
    B. reduce the cost of track repairs
    C. improve train schedules
    D. remove safety hazards

39. Car wheels are *most likely* to squeal when trains are

    A. leaving stations
    B. coasting on straight track
    C. speeding on straight track
    D. running on curved track

40. Track rails which are being unloaded from a work train are generally lifted off rather than dropped in order to prevent   40._____

    A. damaging the rails
    B. damaging the work train
    C. noise
    D. jarring the signals

KEY (CORRECT ANSWERS)

1. B	11. A	21. B	31. C
2. B	12. D	22. C	32. D
3. B	13. A	23. C	33. C
4. C	14. D	24. A	34. C
5. D	15. D	25. C	35. B
6. D	16. D	26. C	36. D
7. B	17. B	27. B	37. C
8. C	18. C	28. A	38. D
9. A	19. D	29. D	39. D
10. B	20. C	30. A	40. A

EXAMINATION SECTION
TEST 1

DIRECTIONS: Each question or incomplete statement is followed by several suggested answers or completions. Select the one that BEST answers the question or completes the statement. *PRINT THE LETTER OF THE CORRECT ANSWER IN THE SPACE AT THE RIGHT.*

QUESTIONS 1-18.

Questions 1-18 on the following page refer to the numbered tools shown below. These tools are not shown to scale.

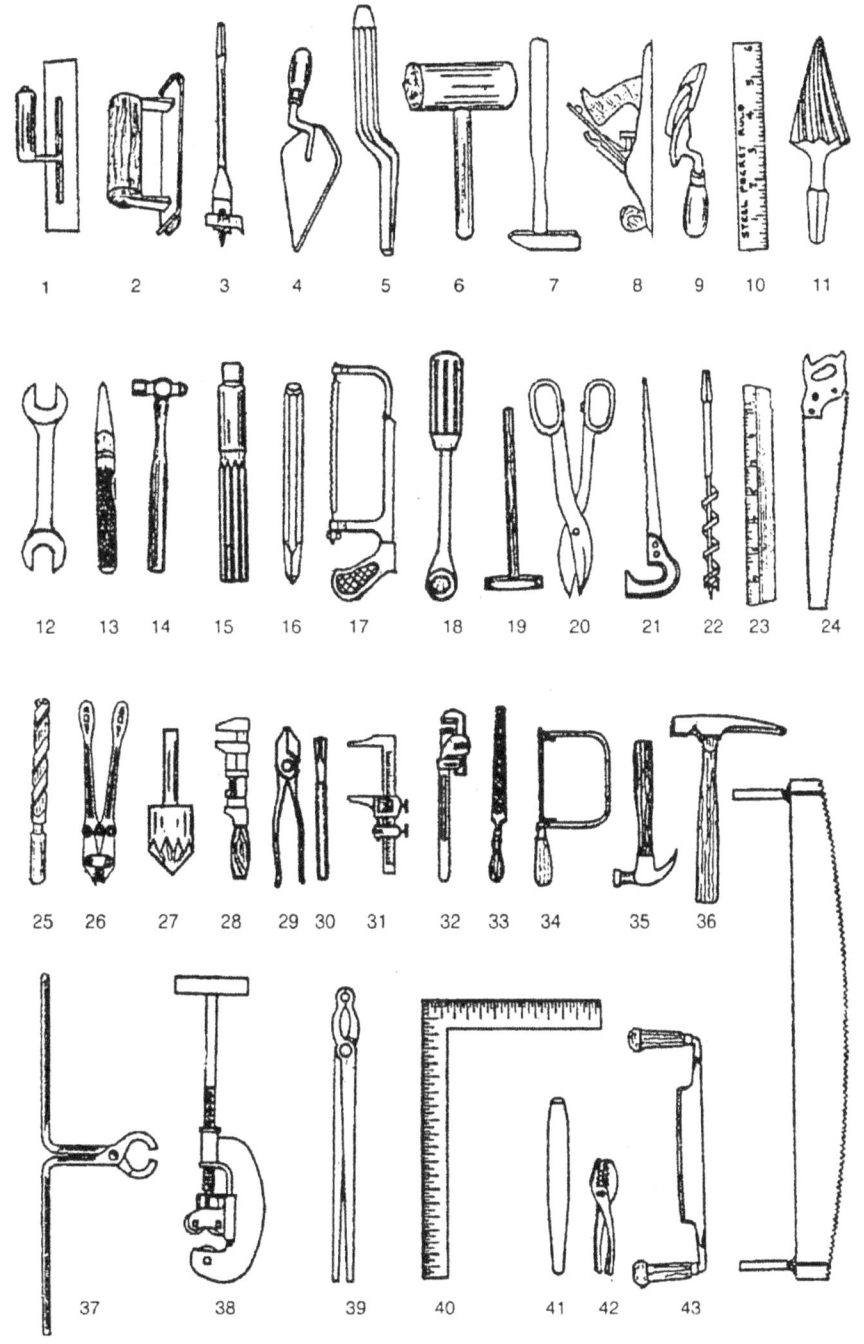

1. To cut a .375" diameter multi-stranded steel cable, you should use tool no.
   A. 5   B. 20   C. 26   D. 37

2. A bracket is to be mounted on a concrete wall by means of screws and lead anchors. To cut holes in the wall for the lead anchors, you should use tool no.
   A. 11   B. 16   C. 30   D. 41

3. To cut a 1 1/2" x 1 1/2" x 1/8" structural steel angle, you should use tool no.
   A. 5   B. 17   C. 20   D. 21

4. To smooth the surface of an unfinished wood board, you should use tool no.
   A. 8   B. 9   C. 17   D. 34

5. To cut off a piece of 1-inch diameter wrought iron pipe from a 12-foot long section of pipe, you should use tool no.
   A. 5   B. 24   C. 34   D. 38

6. To measure a length of tie that is *longer* than 5'6", you should use tool no.
   A. 10   B. 23   C. 31   D. 40

7. It is necessary to bolt two wooden boards together. To drill the holes through the boards, you should use tool no.
   A. 11   B. 16   C. 22   D. 30

8. After cutting off a piece of angle iron, it is desired to make the edges smooth. You should use tool no.
   A. 8   B. 21   C. 33   D. 43

9. To drill a 1/4" diameter bolt hole through two pieces of wrought iron plate, you should use tool no.
   A. 15   B. 22   C. 25   D. 27

10. To tighten a hexagonal brass nut on a 1-inch diamter bolt, you should use tool no.
    A. 18   B. 28   C. 32   D. 42

11. If you want to make a freshly laid cement sidewalk smooth, you should use tool no.
    A. 1   B. 2   C. 9   D. 43

12. To cut a 8" x 8" wooden tie into three *equal* lengths, you should use tool no.
    A. 17   B. 34   C. 43   D. 44

13. To uncouple a two-foot length of threaded 3/4-inch pipe from a pipe coupling, you should use tool no.
    A. 12   B. 28   C. 29   D. 32

14. To cut grooves in a freshly laid cement walkway, you should use tool no.
    A. 1   B. 4   C. 9   D. 36

15. In nailing up a wooden box, a nail may be bent. To remove this bent nail from the box you should use tool no.

    A. 6   B. 7   C. 35   D. 36

16. To line up 3/4" diameter bolt holes in two 1/2" thick steel members, you should use tool no.

    A. 13   B. 16   C. 25   D. 41

17. A pattern is to be cut from a piece of thin brass sheet. You should use tool no.

    A. 17   B. 20   C. 26   D. 29

18. The mortar joints in old brickwork may need to be refilled. To do this work you should use tool no.

    A. 1   B. 2   C. 4   D. 9

QUESTIONS 19-21.
Questions 19 to 21 refer to the drawing shown below.

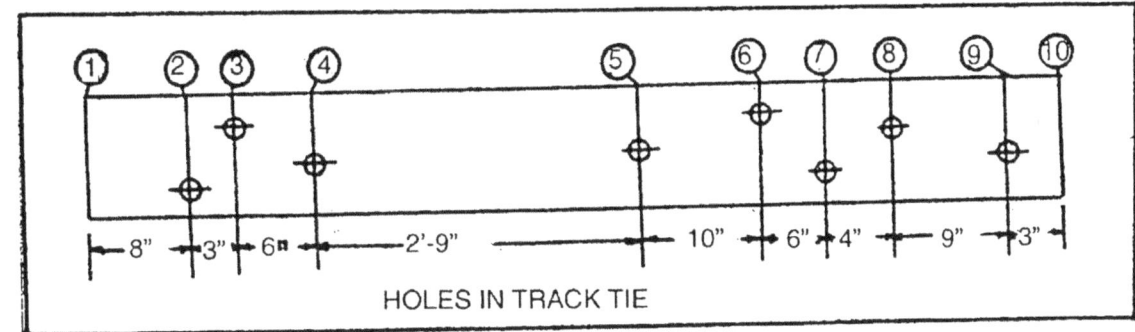

19. The distance from ① to ⑤ is

    A. 2' 9"   B. 3' 6"   C. 4' 2"   D. 5' 1"

20. The distance from ② to is ⑨

    A. 4' 7"   B. 5'11"   C. 6' 2"   D. 7' 3"

21. The length of the tie, ① to is ⑩

    A. 6' 10"   B. 7' 2"   C. 7' 8"   D. 8' 1"

QUESTIONS 22-28.
Questions 22 to 28 refer to the sketches shown to the right of each question.

4 (#1)

22. The circle shown has been divided into five unequal size areas. One-eighth of the area of the full circle is shown by area
    A. V
    B. W
    C. X
    D. Z

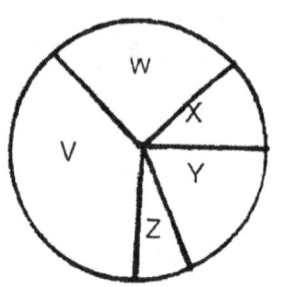

23. For the turnbuckle shown, the number of complete turns of Part 1 required to make the ends of the threaded rods meet is
    A. 2
    B. 5
    C. 10
    D. 20

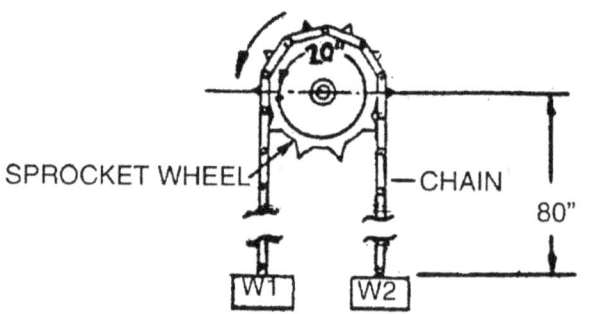

24. The sprocket wheel has a circumference of 20 inches. If the sprocket wheel makes one complete revolution, then weight W2 will be *higher* than weight W1 by
    A. 10"
    B. 20"
    C. 40"
    D. 60"

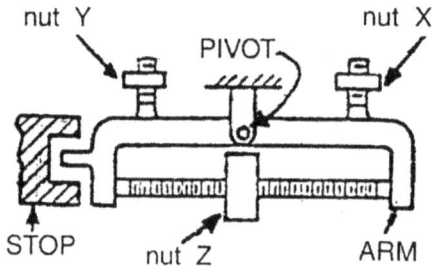

25. The arm of a weighing scale is exactly balanced as shown. In order to rebalance the arm if nut "X" is removed entirely, it will be necessary to move
    A. nut "Y" up
    B. nut "Y" down
    C. nut "Z" toward the right
    D. nut "Z" toward the left

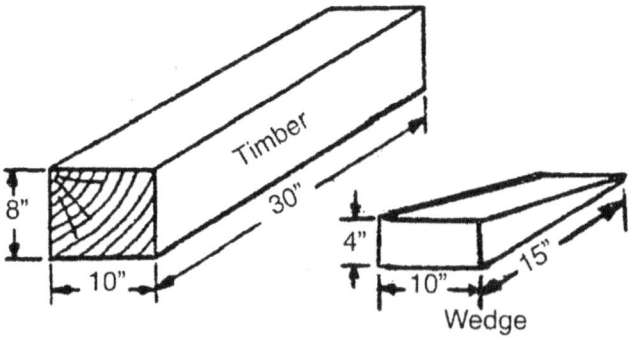

26. The MAXIMUM number of the wedges shown that can be cut from the timber shown is
    A. 4
    B. 8
    C. 12
    D. 16

27. A piece is to be cut out of the angle iron in order to make the right angle bracket shown. Angle "X" should be

   A. 30°
   B. 45°
   C. 90°
   D. 180°

27._____

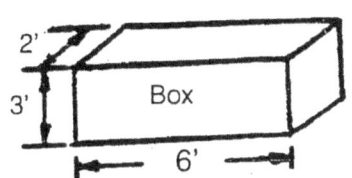

28. The MINIMUM amount of plywood needed to make the fully closed box shown is

   A. 24 sq. ft.
   B. 36 sq. ft.
   C. 60 sq. ft.
   D. 72 sq. ft.

28._____

QUESTIONS 29-32.
Questions 29 to 32 refer to the drawing shown below. Refer to this drawing when answering these questions.

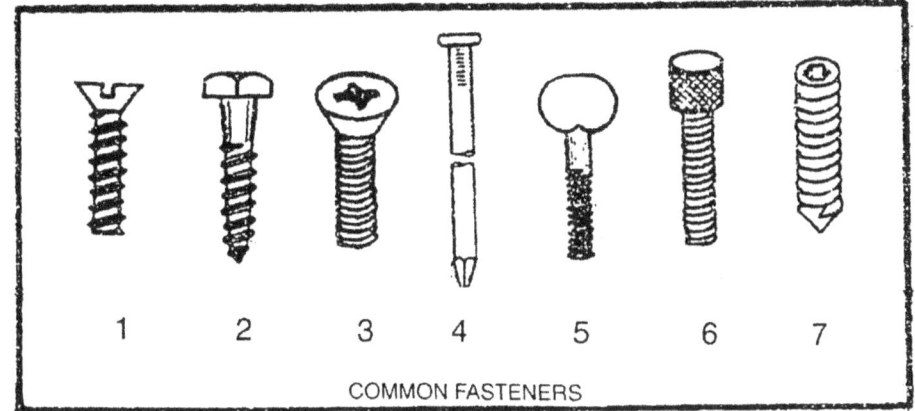

29. The screwdriver shown should be used on number

   A. 1
   B. 2
   C. 3
   D. 6

29._____

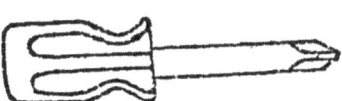

30. The wrench shown should be used on number

   A. 1
   B. 3
   C. 4
   D. 7

30._____

31. The screwdriver shown should be used on number

   A. 1
   B. 2
   C. 3
   D. 5

31._____

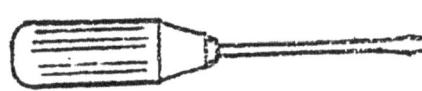

32. The wrench shown should be used on number
    A. 1
    B. 2
    C. 3
    D. 6

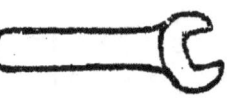

QUESTIONS 33-40.
Questions 33 to 40 refer to the sketches shown to the right of each question.

33. Using only the sizes of washers shown, the LEAST number of washers needed to exactly fill the 1-3/4" space is
    A. 3
    B. 4
    C. 5
    D. 6

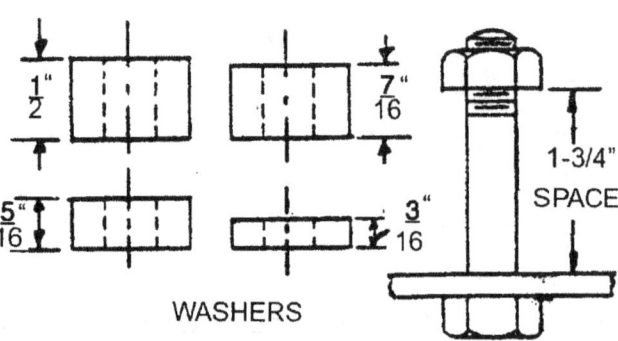

WASHERS

34. The weight is to be raised by means of the rope attached to the truck. If the truck moves forward 36 feet, then the weight will rise _____ feet.
    A. 9
    B. 18
    C. 36
    D. 54

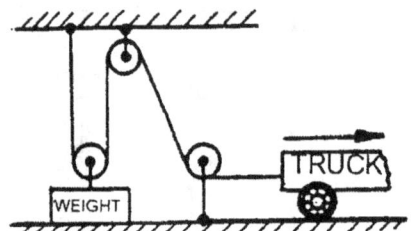

35. The number of complete turns the vise handle must make to fully close the jaws is
    A. 3 1/2
    B. 7
    C. 14
    D. 17 1/2

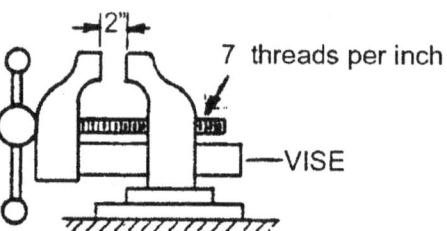

36. The gage reading is most nearly
    A. 30.35
    B. 30.7
    C. 33.5
    D. 37.0

37. If the two slots are the same size, the width of each slot is
    A. 1/2"
    B. 1"
    C. 1 1/2"
    D. 2"

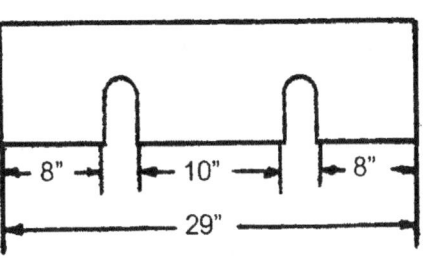

37._____

38. The number of gallons of oil in the drum shown is
    A. 6
    B. 8
    C. 9
    D. 12

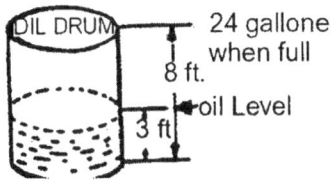

38._____

39. The MINIMUM length of strap iron needed to make the bracket shown is
    A. 32-3/4"
    B. 39 1/2"
    C. 42 1/4"
    D. 45 1/2"

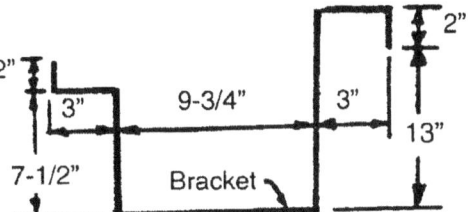

39._____

40. The distance "X" in the figure is
    A. 10'
    B. 12'
    C. 16'
    D. 20'

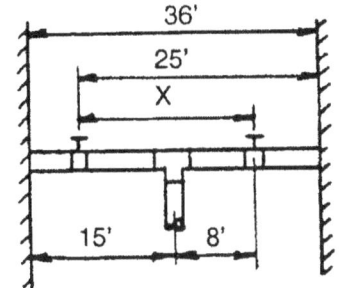

40._____

KEY (CORRECT ANSWERS)

1. C	11. A	21. A	31. A
2. C	12. D	22. C	32. B
3. B	13. D	23. C	33. B
4. A	14. C	24. C	34. B
5. D	15. C	25. C	35. C
6. B	16. D	26. B	36. D
7. C	17. B	27. C	37. C
8. C	18. C	28. D	38. C
9. C	19. C	29. C	39. C
10. B	20. B	30. D	40. B

TEST 2

DIRECTIONS: Each question or incomplete statement is followed by several suggested answers or completions. Select the one that BEST answers the question or completes the statement. *PRINT THE LETTER OF THE CORRECT ANSWER IN THE SPACE AT THE RIGHT.*

1. The MOST important reason for the Transit Authority rule that unauthorized employees are prohibited from entering on the subway track is that such entry

    A. is unlawful
    B. sets a bad example for others
    C. is dangerous
    D. delays trains

    1.____

2. If it costs $65 for 20 feet of subway rail, the cost of 150 feet of this rail will be

    A. $487.50   B. $512.00   C. $589.50   D. $650.00

    2.____

3. When summoning an ambulance for an injured person, it is MOST important to give the

    A. time of the accident
    B. cause of the accident
    C. name of the injured person
    D. location of the injured person

    3.____

4. Transit authority workers are advised to report injuries caused by nails, no matter how slight the injury.
   The MOST important reason for this rule is that this type of injury

    A. is caused by violating some safety rule
    B. can only be the result of carelessness
    C. generally is overlooked
    D. may result in serious infection

    4.____

QUESTIONS 5-14.
Questions 5 to 14 are based on the sketch below showing a pile of track ties. Refer to this sketch when answering these questions.

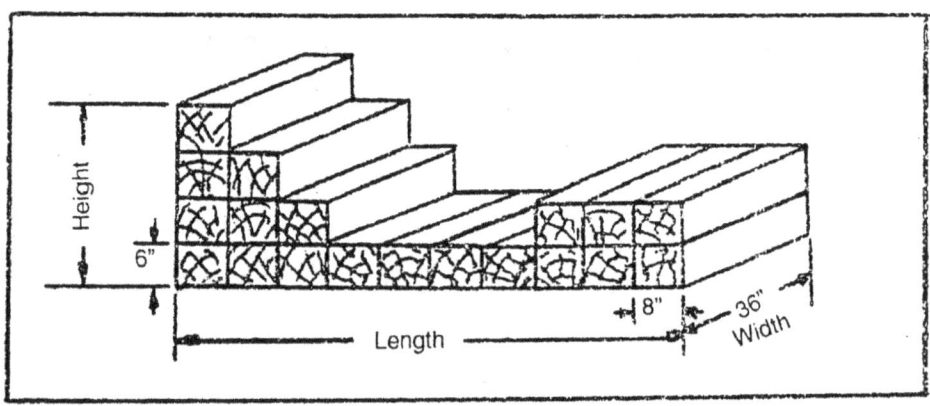

5. The TOTAL number of ties shown is 5.____
   A. 15   B. 17   C. 19   D. 21

6. At its HIGHEST, the pile is 6.____
   A. 6" high   B. 12" high   C. 18" high   D. 24" high

7. At its LOWEST, the pile is 7.____
   A. 6" high   B. 8" high   C. 12" high   D. 16" high

8. The SMALLEST overall dimension of the pile is the 8.____
   A. height   B. length   C. width   D. perimeter

9. The length of the pile is 9.____
   A. 36"   B. 48"   C. 60"   D. 80"

10. The pile is *greater* in 10.____
    A. width than in length
    B. height than in length
    C. height than in width
    D. length than in height

11. To reduce the pile shown to a maximum height of 12", the number of ties which should be removed is 11.____
    A. 3   B. 6   C. 9   D. 12

12. The pile shown can be filled solid to an even height of four layers by adding 12.____
    A. 4 ties   B. 15 ties   C. 21 ties   D. 24 ties

13. The total number of ties which do NOT rest directly on the ground is 13.____
    A. 7   B. 8   C. 9   D. 12

14. The size of each tie is 14.____
    A. 6" x 6" by 3' 0"
    B. 6" x 8" by 3' 0"
    C. 6" x 8" by 2' 6"
    D. 8" x 8" by 2' 6"

15. If you earn $10.20 per hour and time and one-half for working over 40 hours, your gross salary for a week in which you worked 42 hours would be 15.____
    A. 408.00   B. 428.40   C. 438.60   D. 770.80

16. A drill bit, used to drill holes in track ties, has a diameter of 0.75 inches. When expressed as a fraction, the diameter of this drill bit is 16.____
    A. 1/4"   B. 3/8"   C. 1/2"   D. 3/4"

17. A "reamer" should be used by a trackman in order to 17.____
    A. line up holes
    B. drill holes
    C. enlarge existing holes slightly
    D. rethread track bolts

18. Transit authority employees are cautioned NOT to use water to put out fires in electrical equipment mainly because water

    A. will cause sensitive electrical parts to corrode
    B. will cause electrical shorts and result in blowing of fuses
    C. may conduct the electrical current and create a shock hazard
    D. may generate high-temperature steam

19. When repair work is being done on the elevated rapid transit structure, canvas spreads are suspended under the working area mainly to

    A. prevent loss of tools
    B. discourage crowds
    C. protect the structure
    D. protect pedestrians

20. Transit authority employees must give notice of their intention to be absent from work several hours before they are scheduled to report for duty.
    The MOST logical reason for having this rule is that

    A. it allows time for assigning a substitute
    B. it allows time to send a doctor
    C. it has a nuisance value in discouraging absences
    D. the employee's time record can be corrected in advance

21. The sum of 4-1/16, 5 1/4, 3-5/8 and 4-7/16 is

    A. 17-3/16   B. 17 1/4   C. 17-5/16   D. 17-3/8

22. The edges of the top steps on some subway stations are painted yellow in order to

    A. make them less slippery
    B. show up the dirt
    C. aid in keeping them clean
    D. make them stand out

23. In order to prevent slipping, the bottoms of ladder side rails are often fitted with

    A. lifters   B. locks   C. wedges   D. shoes

24. The number of cubic feet of concrete it takes to fill a form 10 feet long, 3 feet wide and 6 inches deep is

    A. 12   B. 15   C. 20   D. 180

QUESTIONS 25-31.
Questions 25-31 are to be answered *solely* on the basis of the passage below.

OPEN-END WRENCHES

Solid, non-adjustable wrenches with openings in one or both ends are called open-end wrenches. Wrenches with small openings are usually shorter than wrenches with large openings. This proportions the lever advantage of the wrench to the bolt or stud and helps prevet wrench breakage or damage to the bolt or stud.

Open-end wrenches may have their jaws parallel to the handle or at angles anywhere up to 90 degrees. The average angle is 15 degrees. This angular displacement variation permits selection of a wrench suited for places where there is room to make only a part of a complete turn of a nut or bolt. Handles are usually straight, but may be curved. Those with curved handles are called S-wrenches. Other open-end wrenches may have offset handles. This allows the head to reach nut or bolt heads that are sunk below the surface.

There are a few basic rules that you should keep in mind when using wrenches. They are:

    I. ALWAYS use a wrench that fits the nut properly. Otherwise the wrench may slip, or the nut may be damaged.
    II. Keep wrenches clean and free from oil. Otherwise they may slip, resulting in possible serious injury to you or damage to the work.
    III. Do NOT increase the leverage of a wrench by placing a pipe over the handle. Increased leverage may damage the wrench or the work.

25. Open-end wrenches

    A. are adjustable
    B. are solid
    C. always have openings at both ends
    D. are always S-shaped

26. Wrench proportions are such that wrenches with

    A. larger openings have shorter handles
    B. smaller opernings have longer handles
    C. larger openings have longer handles
    D. smaller openings have thicker handles

27. The average angle between the jaws and the handle of a wrench is _____ degrees.

    A. 0   B. 15   C. 22   D. 90

28. Offset handles are intended for use *mainly* with

    A. offset nuts
    B. bolts having fine threads
    C. nuts sunk below the surface
    D. bolts that permit limited swing

29. The wrench which is selected should fit the nut properly because this

    A. prevents distorting the wrench
    B. insures use of all wrench sizes
    C. avoids damaging the nut
    D. overstresses the bolt

30. Oil on wrenches is

    A. *good*, because it prevents rust
    B. *good,* because it permits easier turning
    C. *bad,* because the wrench may slip off the nut
    D. *bad,* because the oil may spoil the work

31. Extending the handle of a wrench by slipping a piece of pipe over it is considered

    A. *good*, because it insures a tight nut
    B. *good*, because less effort is needed to loosen a nut
    C. *bad*, because the wrench may be damaged
    D. *bad*, because the amount of tightening can not be controlled

32. Transit authority employees who are required to walk on the subway tracks are cautioned to walk opposite to the direction of traffic on the track.
    This is required because the employee

    A. can see any obstacle more clearly
    B. is more likely to see an approaching train
    C. will be seen more readily by the motorman
    D. is better able to judge the speed of an approaching train

33. Good safety practices require that tools should always be kept in good condition.
    The MOST important reason for this is that

    A. perfect tools make a perfect job
    B. defective tools are dangerous
    C. such tools are expensive
    D. less effort is then needed to use them

34. Some of the metal fittings used on track work are galvanized. The MAIN purpose of such galvanizing is to make

    A. welding easier
    B. drilling easier
    C. the fitting rust-resistant
    D. the fitting stronger

35. Steel is commonly cut by a "burning torch" that is fed by two tanks of gas. One of these gases is acetylene and the other is

    A. hydrogen   B. nitrogen   C. propane   D. oxygen

36. Using compressed air to blow dirt from your clothing is

    A. *bad*, since this is expensive
    B. *bad*, since dirt may be blown into your eyes
    C. *good*, since it keeps you clean and presentable
    D. *good*, since this is an effective way of removing small particles

37. Three dozen shovels were purchased for use. If the shovels were used at the rate of nine a week, the number of weeks that the three dozen lasted was

    A. 3   B. 4   C. 9   D. 12

38. Assume that you earn $20,000 per year. If twenty percent of your pay is deducted for taxes, social security and pension, your weekly take-home pay will be most nearly

    A. $280   B. $308   C. $328   D. $344

39. Assume it is necessary for you to work with your hands under a piece of heavy eq'uipment while a fellow worker lifts one end with a crow bar.
In this case the SAFEST procedure would be to

    A. wear heavy gloves
    B. work as fast as possible
    C. insert temporary blocks to support the piece
    D. Use one hand to work and one to hold up the equipment

39.____

40. Before stepping on a subway track, you should

    A. find out if the power is on
    B. turn off your lantern
    C. look up and down the track
    D. notify the transit police

40.____

KEY (CORRECT ANSWERS)

1.	C	11.	A	21.	D	31.	C
2.	A	12.	C	22.	D	32.	B
3.	D	13.	C	23.	D	33.	B
4.	D	14.	B	24.	B	34.	C
5.	C	15.	C	25.	B	35.	D
6.	D	16.	D	26.	C	36.	B
7.	A	17.	C	27.	B	37.	B
8.	A	18.	C	28.	C	38.	B
9.	D	19.	D	29.	C	39.	C
10.	D	20.	A	30.	C	40.	C

EXAMINATION SECTION
TEST 1

DIRECTIONS: Each question or incomplete statement is followed by several suggested answers or completions. Select the one that BEST answers the question or completes the Statement. *PRINT THE LETTER OF THE CORRECT ANSWER IN THE SPACE AT THE RIGHT.*

Questions 1-16.

DIRECTIONS: Questions on these tools are to be found on the following page. (These tools are not shown to scale.)

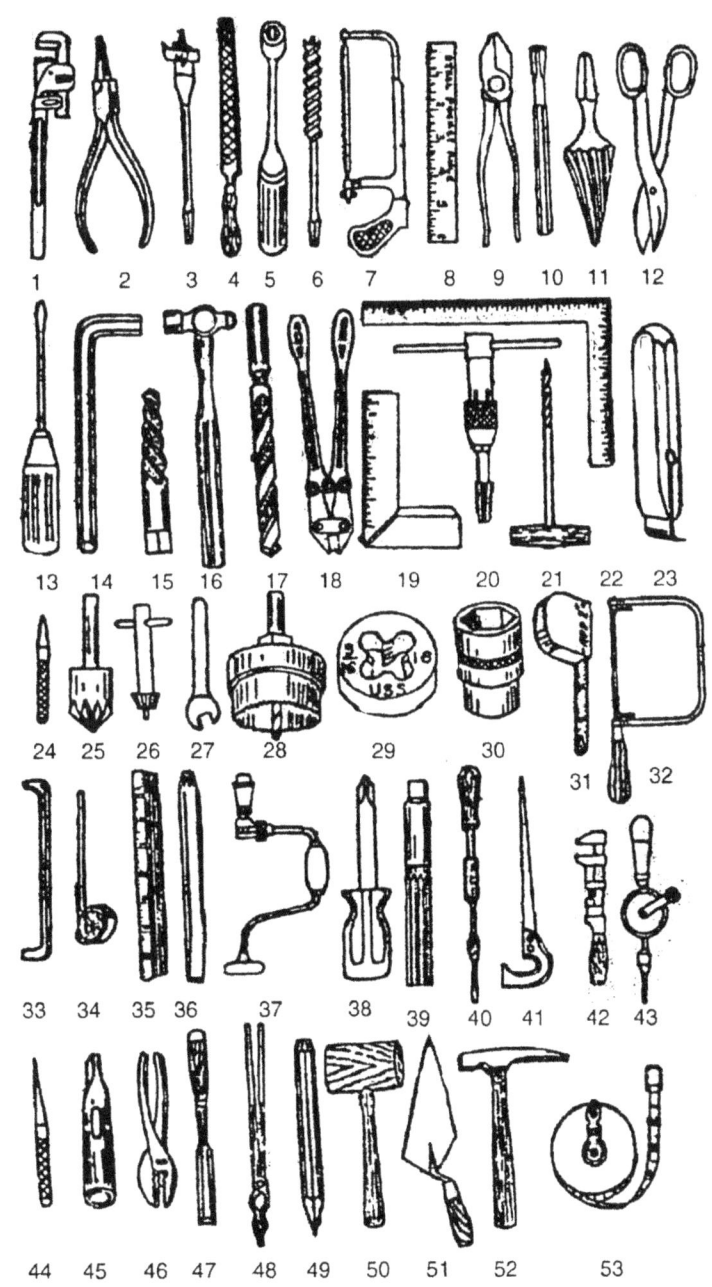

NOTE: Questions 1 through 16 refer to the tools shown on the preceding page. (The *numbers* in the choices refer to the *numbers* beneath the tools.)

1. To remove cutting burrs from the inside of a pipe, you should use tool number
   A. 4 B. 7 C. 11 D. 15

2. To join lengths of chrome-plated pipe, you should use tool
   A. 1 B. 34 C. 42 D. 46

3. To countersink a hole in a plywood shelf, you should use tool number
   A. 3 B. 11 C. 25 D. 28

4. To tighten plumbing fixtures having hexagonal ends, you should use tool number
   A. 1 B. 9 C. 34 D. 42

5. To lift a hot rivet from the furnace, you should use tool number
   A. 2 B. 18 C. 46 D. 48

6. To cut a 3/8 inch steel cable, you should use tool number
   A. 2 B. 12 C. 18 D. 41

7. To tighten a lag screw, you should use tool number
   A. 1 B. 27 C. 33 D. 46

8. To make holes for sheet metal screws, you should use tool number
   A. 3 B. 11 C. 21 D. 43

9. To remove a broken-off piece of a small-diameter pipe from a fitting, you should use tool number
   A. 11 B. 15 C. 17 D. 39

10. The term "16 oz." should be applied to tool number
    A. 1 B. 12 C. 16 D. 42

11. The term "coping" should be applied to tool number
    A. 7 B. 28 C. 32 D. 41

12. The term "die" should be applied to tool number
    A. 11 B. 20 C. 29 D. 39

13. The term "star" should be applied to tool number
    A. 3 B. 10 C. 25 D. 28

14. If tool number 6 bears the mark "5," this tool should be used to drill holes having a *diameter* of
    A. 5/32" B. 5/16" C. 5/8" D. 5"

15. The marking "18" on tool number 29 refers to the   15._____

    A. maximum diameter of rod   B. minimum diameter of rod
    C. number of threads per inch   D. degree of taper of threads

16. If the marking on the blade of tool number 7 reads: "12-32," the 32 refers to the   16._____

    A. length
    B. thickness
    C. weight
    D. number of teeth per inch

17. If a maintainer is chipping concrete with a pneumatic hammer, the MOST important   17._____
    safety precaution for this maintainer to follow is to wear

    A. a hard hat   B. heavy shoes
    C. goggles   D. a long-sleeved shirt

18. Forms for concrete are coated with oil because the oil   18._____

    A. makes the finished surface smoother
    B. imparts a grayish color to the concrete
    C. reduces the time required for the concrete to set
    D. makes it easier to remove the forms after the concrete has set

19. Artificial respiration should be applied when an accident victim shows signs of   19._____

    A. excessive bleeding   B. rapid breathing
    C. bad scalding   D. breathing difficulties

20. Shop workers are often warned against wearing rings during working hours MAINLY   20._____
    because of the danger

    A. of theft   B. of loss
    C. to machinery   D. to the employee

21. The MAIN purpose of using lightweight concrete for floor construction is to   21._____

    A. improve insulation
    B. reduce the weight
    C. furnish a smooth surface
    D. make floor maintenance easier

22. The rules state that employees should not make any statements concerning transit acci- 22._____
    dents except to the proper officials. The PROBABLE reason for this rule is to

    A. prevent lawsuits
    B. keep the facts from the public
    C. avoid conflicting testimony
    D. prevent unofficial statements from being accepted as official

23. The SAFEST way of handling a bank of lights which operate on third rail power, is to 23._____

    A. connect the negative lead to the signal rail
    B. connect the negative lead to the third rail
    C. connect the positive lead before connecting the negative lead
    D. disconnect the positive lead before disconnecting the negative lead

4. (#1)

Questions 24-31.
DIRECTIONS: In questions 24 through 31, the item referred to is shown
to the right of the question.

24. The distance "Y" is
    A. 12 inches
    B. 13 inches
    C. 16 inches
    D. 19 inches

24. ...

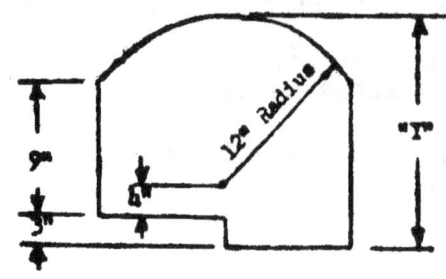

25. The tank now contains 24 gallons of water.
    If 8 gallons are removed, the present wa-
    ter height of 9" will be reduced to
    A. 2 inches
    B. 4 inches
    C. 6 inches
    D. 8 inches

25. ...

26. The volume of the bar, in cubic
    inches, is
    A. 30
    B. 36
    C. 60
    D. 66

26. ...

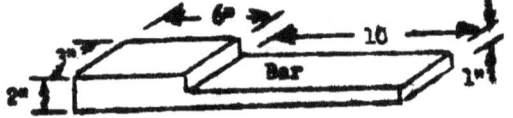

27. The distance "Y" on the plate is
    A. 2 1/2 inches
    B. 3 1/2 inches
    C. 4 1/2 inches
    D. 5 1/2 inches

27. ...

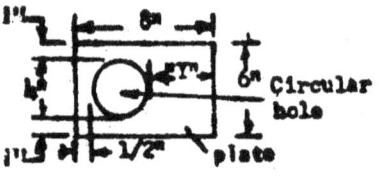

28. The areas of the cross-hatched
    section of the pattern is
    A. 48 square inches
    B. 72 square inches
    C. 96 square inches
    D. 144 square inches

28. ...

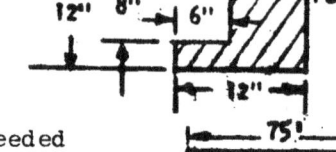

29. The length of chain-link fence needed
    to enclose the yard is
    A. 330 ft.   B. 380 ft.
    C. 430 ft.   D. 480 ft.

29. ...

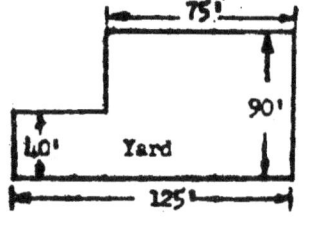

30. The reading on the weighing scale
    should be APPROXIMATELY
    A. zero   B. 10 lbs.
    C. 20 lbs.   D. 30 lbs.

30. ...

31. The strap-iron bracked shown is
    to support a ventilating duct.
    The length of strap needed be-
    fore bending is
    A. 31 3/4 inches
    B. 38 1/2 inches
    C. 41 1/4 inches
    D. 44 1/2 inches

31. ...

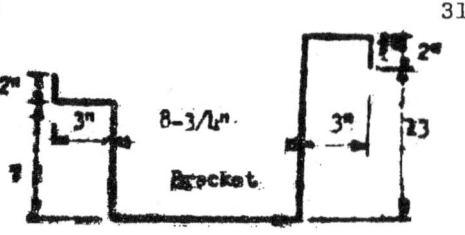

Questions 32-40.
DIRECTIONS: Questions on this plumbing sketch appear on the next page.

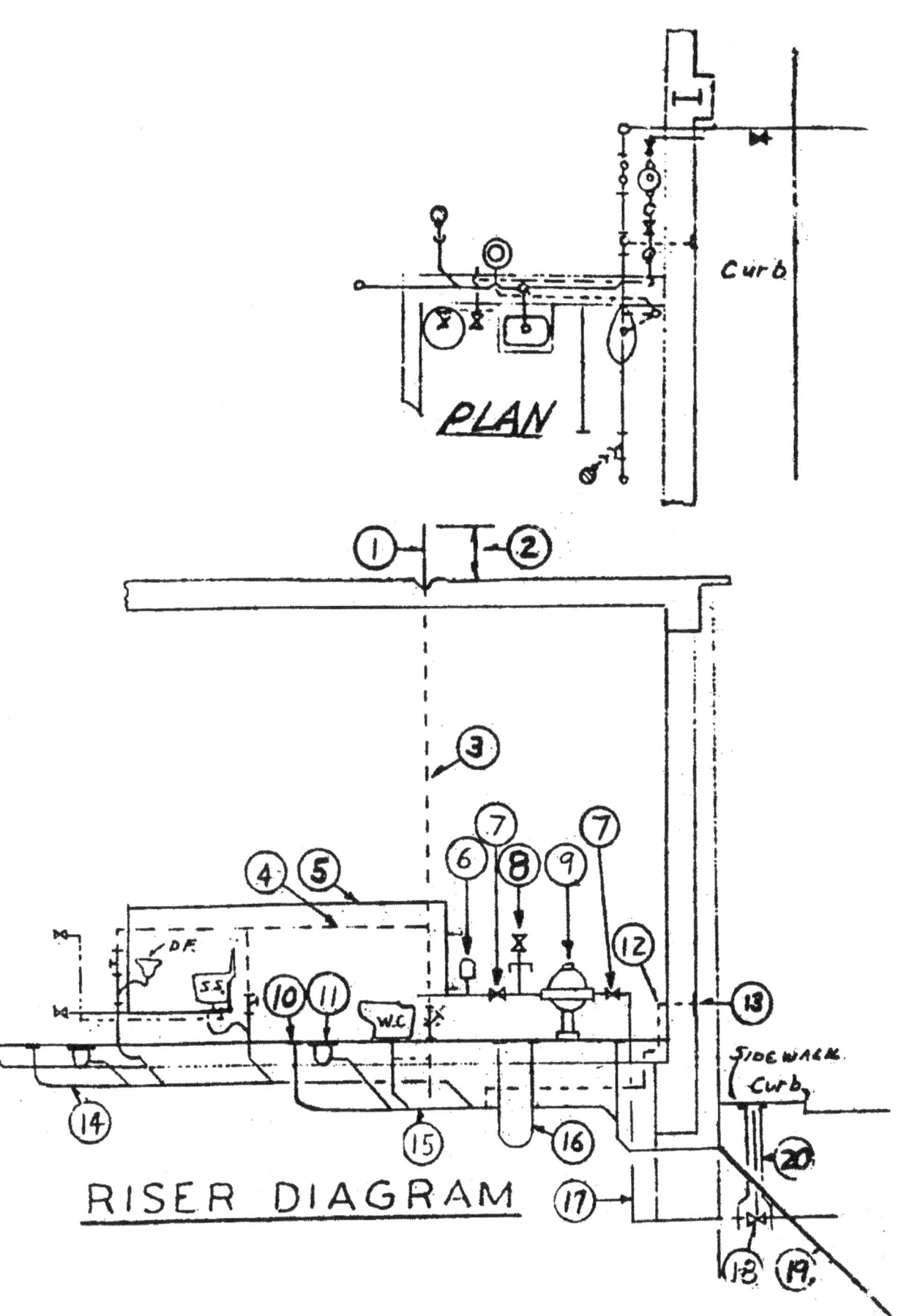

NOTE: Questions 32 through 40 refer to the plumbing sketch on the preceding page. Refer to this sketch when answering these questions.

32. The vent stack ③ should be made of

    A. cast iron
    B. galvanized iron
    C. copper
    D. plastic

33. The line marked ⑤ is a

    A. soil line
    B. vent line
    C. hot water line
    D. cold water line

34. The purpose of the valves ⑦ on either side of the meter is to

    A. reduce water hammer
    B. permit easy removal of the meter
    C. allow by-passing the meter
    D. adjust water flow

35. The purpose of the test tee at ⑧ is to

    A. determine the purity of the water
    B. establish the proper water pressure
    C. check the accuracy of the meter
    D. apply pressure to test the piping

36. The plumbing fitting in the floor at ⑩ is a

    A. trap
    B. valve
    C. clean out
    D. inlet

37. The fresh-air inlet plate at ⑬ is a part of the

    A. room ventilation
    B. air conditioning
    C. soil line
    D. vent line

38. The plumbing fitting at ⑯ is a

    A. trap
    B. vent
    C. meter
    D. floor drain

39. The pipe at ⑲ is a

    A. hot water line
    B. cold water line
    C. soil line
    D. vent line

40. The purpose of the curb box at ⑳ is to permit

    A. checking the water flor
    B. checking the water pressure
    C. the water to be shut off
    D. determination of water purity

KEY (CORRECT ANSWERS)

1. C	11. C	21. B	31. C
2. B	12. C	22. D	32. A
3. C	13. B	23. D	33. D
4. D	14. B	24. D	34. B
5. D	15. C	25. C	35. C
6. C	16. D	26. D	36. C
7. B	17. C	27. B	37. D
8. D	18. D	28. C	38. A
9. B	19. D	29. C	39. C
10. C	20. D	30. D	40. C

TEST 2

DIRECTIONS: Each question or incomplete statement is followed by several suggested answers or completions. Select the one that BEST answers the question or completes the statement.

1. Maintenance workers are required to report defective equipment to their superiors even when the maintenance of the particular equipment is handled by another department. The PURPOSE of this rule is to

    A. keep employees alert
    B. reward employees who keep their eyes open
    C. pinpoint what department is falling down on its job
    D. have repairs made before serious trouble occurs

2. The MOST important reason for training employees is to

    A. satisfy their ego
    B. satisfy the unions
    C. improve the employees' ability to do a good job
    D. keep the supervisory personnel on their toes

3. The BEST first aid for an unconscious person lying on the ground is to

    A. sit him up
    B. cover his body with a blanket
    C. give him something to drink
    D. remove his outer clothing to keep him cool

4. The rules prohibit the use of the telephones for personal calls. The MOST important reason for this rule is that such personal calls

    A. cost the Authority money
    B. require additional telephone operators
    C. may tie up the telephone when needed for Authority business
    D. take the men away from their work

5. Of the following, the MAIN purpose of a safety training program is to

    A. fix the blame for accidents
    B. describe accidents which have occurred
    C. make the men aware of the basic causes of accidents
    D. maintain job progress under unsafe working conditions

6. Sharp edged tools should not be carried in a maintainer's pocket MAINLY because the

    A. tool's edge may become damaged
    B. tool is more readily lost
    C. tool may injure the maintainer
    D. maintainer may take the tool back to the locker room

Questions 7-13.

DIRECTIONS: Questions 7 through 13 refer to the sketches below. In answering these questions refer to the appropriate sketch.

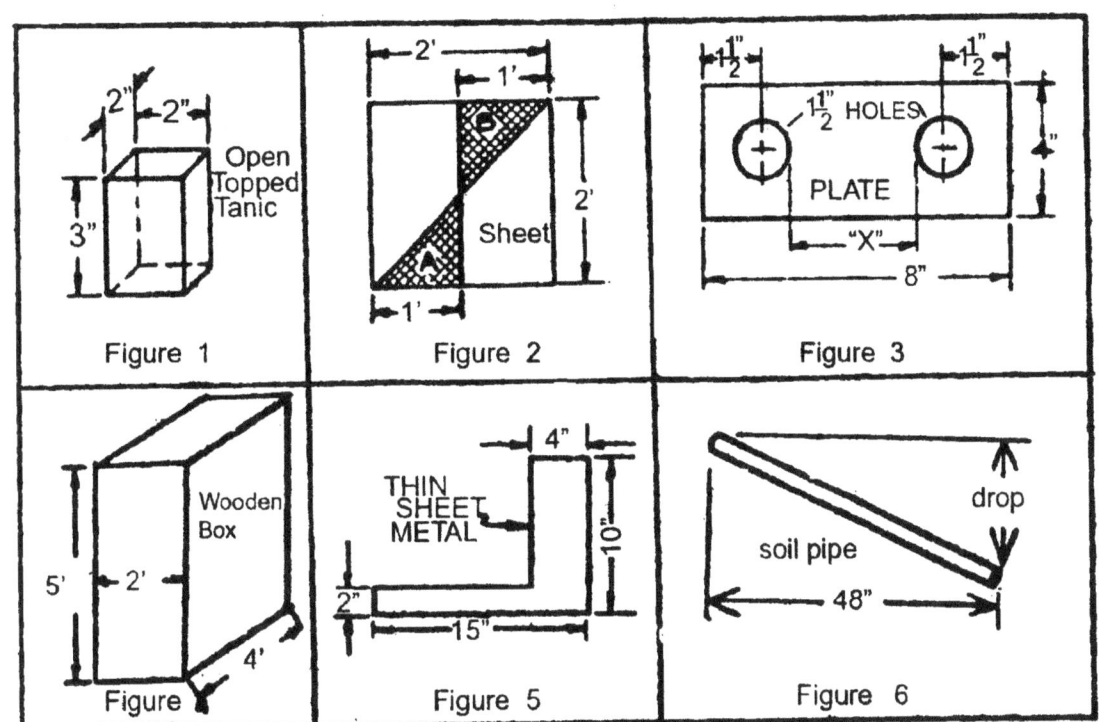

7. The MAXIMUM amount of water that the tank in Figure 1 can hold is

    A. 4 cu.in.   B. 6 cu.in.   C. 8 cu.in.   D. 12 cu.in.

7._____

8. The external surface area of sheet metal used to make the tank in Figure 1 is

    A. 12 sq.in.   B. 24 sq.in.   C. 28 sq.in.   D. 32 sq.in.

8._____

9. The MAXIMUM number of triangular pieces, equal in area to A or B in Figure 2, which can be cut from the full sheet is

    A. 4   B. 6   C. 8   D. 10

9._____

10. The distance "X" between the circular holes in Figure 3 is

    A. 2"   B. 3"   C. 3 1/2"   D. 5 1/2"

10._____

11. The MINIMUM amount of plywood needed to make the closed wood-en box in Figure 4 is

    A. 56.sq.ft.   B. 60 sq.ft.   C. 76 sq.ft.   D. 80 sq.ft.

11._____

12. The surface area of the sheet metal shape shown in Figure 5 is

    A. 42 sq.in.   B. 52 sq.in.   C. 62 sq.in.   D. 70 sq.in.

12._____

13. If the soil pipe in Figure 6 has a pitch of 1/2" per foot, the TOTAL drop in a horizontal run of 48 feet is

    A. 2 feet   B. 3 feet   C. 4 feet   D. 5 feet

13._____

Questions 14-24.

DIRECTIONS: In questions 14 through 24, the item referred to is shown to the right of the question.

14. The bolt shown should be used
    A. in foundations
    B. in cement curbs
    C. to connect rails
    D. to connect girders

14.____

15. The screw shown is called a
    A. set screw
    B. anchor screw
    C. lag screw
    D. toggle screw

15.____

16. The anchor shown should be used in a
    A. wood post
    B. concrete wall
    C. plaster wall
    D. gypsum block wall

16.____

17. The wrench shown is called a(n)
    A. monkey wrench
    B. Allen wrench
    C. "L" wrench
    D. socket wrench

17.____

18. The anchor shown should be used in a
    A. concrete wall
    B. veneer wall
    C. plaster wall
    D. brick wall

18.____

19. The cutter shown should be used on
    A. pipes
    B. cables
    C. re-bars
    D. bolts

19.____

20. The saw shown is called a
    A. coping saw
    B. cross-cut saw
    C. hack saw
    D. back saw

20.____

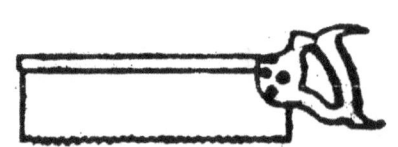

21. The tool shown is a
    A. "D" clamp
    B. "C" clamp
    C. pipe vise
    D. metal vise

21.____

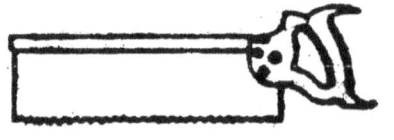

22. The tool shown is a
    A. hawk
    B. trowel
    C. screed
    D. joiner

22.____

23. The tool shown is called a
    A. try square
    B. T-bevel
    C. miter box
    D. miter square

23.____

24. The tool shown should be used to
    A. make grooves in side walks
    B. turn lead bends
    C. make copper bends
    D. finish brick joints

24.____

25. All employees are required to give their names and badge numbers, without delay or argument, to any passenger who may request this information. The MAIN reason for this rule is that

    A. the subwsys are publicly owned
    B. essentially the passenger is the employer
    C. the passenger may be a policeman in plain clothes
    D. it makes for better public relations

25.____

26. The MAIN purpose of weep holes in cavity wall construction is to

    A. permit expansion
    B. help cure the concrete
    C. insulate the walls
    D. drain off moisture

26.____

27. The information in an accident report which may be MOST useful in decreasing the number of similar accidents is the

    A. number of people involved
    B. cause of the accident
    C. extent of the injuries sustained
    D. time the accident happened

27.____

28. The transit police must be notified first whenever an ambulance is needed. The MAIN reason for this rule is to

    A. prevent duplication of calls
    B. prevent ambulances from being sent to non-transit accidents
    C. allow the police to determine the need of an ambulance
    D. insure that the police are on hand

28.____

29. The MAIN purpose of giving employees instructions in first aid is to

    A. reduce the number of accidents
    B. save money on compensation causes
    C. eliminate the need for calling doctors
    D. enable them to provide emergency aid if needed

29.____

30. When steel is given two coats of paint, a different color is used for the second coat MAINLY to

   A. insure that two coats were actually applied
   B. insure full coverage by the second coat
   C. prevent electrolysis
   D. avoid painting in the field

Questions 31-40.

DIRECTIONS: Questions 31 through 40 deal with relationships between sets of figures. For each question, select that choice (A, or B, or C, or D) which has the SAME relationship to Figure 3 that Figure 2 has to Figure 1.

SAMPLE: Study Figures 1 and 2 in the SAMPLE. Notice that Figure 1 has been turned clockwise 1/4 of a turn to get Figure 2. Taking Figure 3 and turning it clockwise 1/4 of a turn, we get choice A, the correct answer.

KEY (CORRECT ANSWERS)

1. D	11. C	21. B	31. C
2. C	12. C	22. B	32. B
3. B	13. A	23. C	33. D
4. C	14. A	24. A	34. A
5. C	15. C	25. D	35. B
6. C	16. B	26. D	36. C
7. D	17. B	27. B	37. A
8. C	18. C	28. A	38. B
9. C	19. A	29. D	39. B
10. C	20. D	30. B	40. D

EXAMINATION SECTION
TEST 1

DIRECTIONS: Each question or incomplete statement is followed by several suggested answers or completions. Select the one that BEST answers the question or completes the statement. *PRINT THE LETTER OF THE CORRECT ANSWER IN THE SPACE AT THE RIGHT.*

Questions 1-17.

DIRECTIONS: Questions 1 through 17 are to be answered on the basis of the tools shown below and on the following page. The numbers in the answers refer to the numbers beneath the tools.

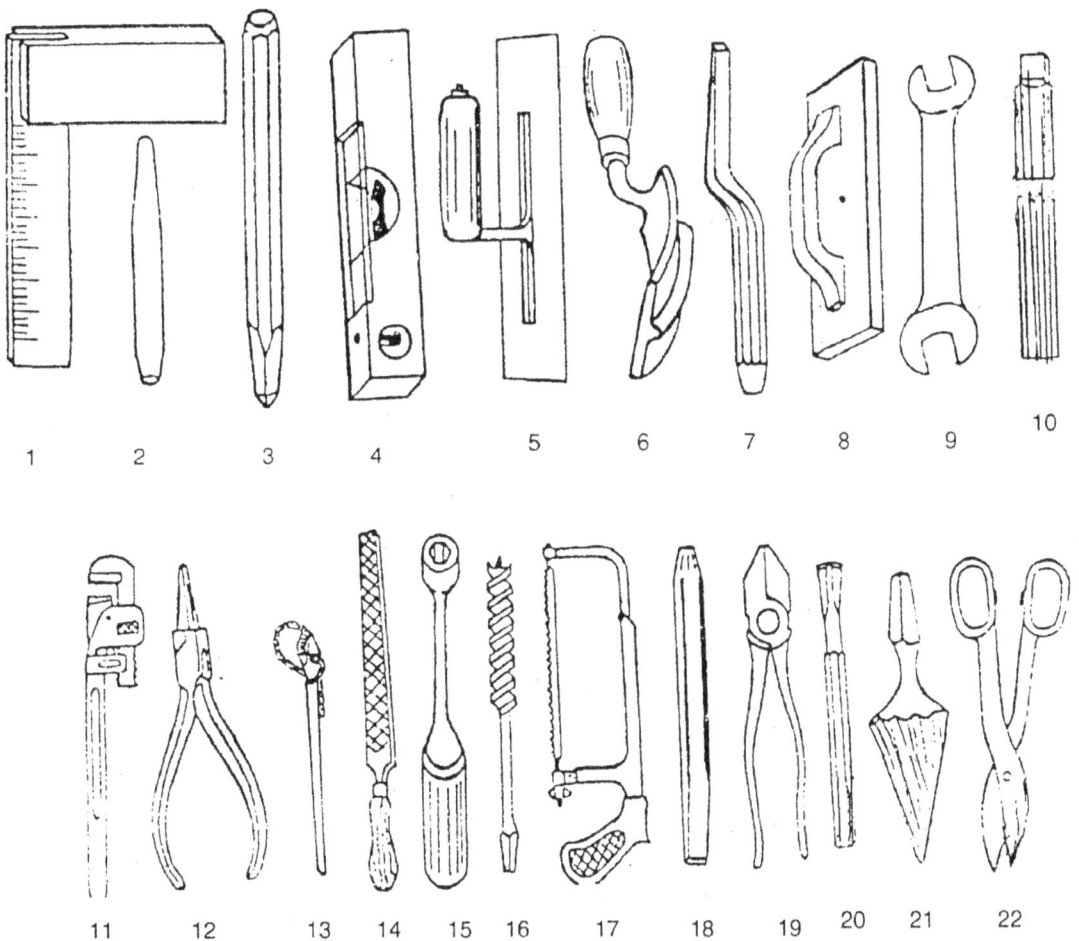

2 (#1)

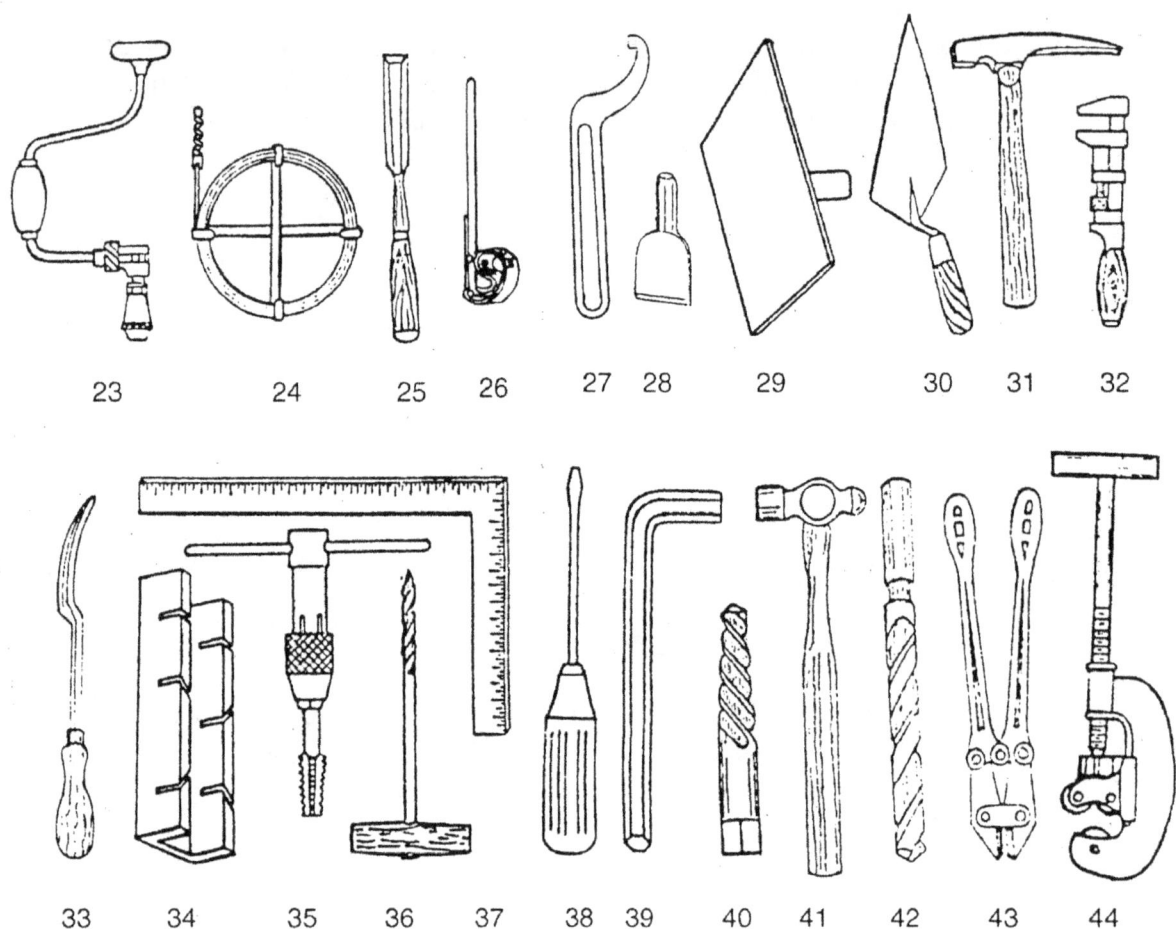

1. To tighten an elbow onto a threaded pipe, a mechanic should use tool number
   A. 9   B. 11   C. 26   D. 32

2. To cut grooves in newly poured cement, a mechanic should use tool number
   A. 5   B. 6   C. 28   D. 29

3. To *caulk* a lead joint, a mechanic should use tool number
   A. 7   B. 10   C. 25   D. 33

4. The term *snips* should be applied by a mechanic to tool number
   A. 12   B. 22   C. 36   D. 43

5. To slightly enlarge an existing 17/32" diameter hole in a metal plate, a mechanic should use tool number
   A. 3   B. 10   C. 14   D. 35

6. The term *snake* should be applied by a mechanic to tool number
   A. 21   B. 23   C. 24   D. 40

7. If the threaded portion of a 1/2" brass pipe breaks off inside a gate valve, the piece should be removed with tool number

   A. 15　　B. 35　　C. 39　　D. 40

8. To cut a face brick into a bat, a mechanic should use tool number

   A. 3　　B. 18　　C. 25　　D. 28

9. A mechanic should cut a 3" x 2" x 3/16" angle iron with tool number

   A. 3　　B. 17　　C. 22　　D. 43

10. A mechanic should tighten a chrome-plated water supply pipe by using tool number

    A. 11　　B. 19　　C. 26　　D. 32

11. The term *hawk* should be applied by a mechanic to tool number

    A. 28　　B. 29　　C. 30　　D. 33

12. If your co-worker asks you to pass him the *star* drill, you should hand him tool number

    A. 16　　B. 20　　C. 40　　D. 42

13. After threading a 1" diameter piece of pipe, a mechanic should debur the inside by using tool number

    A. 14　　B. 21　　C. 36　　D. 40

14. A mechanic should apply the term *float* to tool number

    A. 4　　B. 6　　C. 8　　D. 28

15. If a mechanic has to cut a dozen 15-inch lengths of 3/4-inch steel pipe for spacers, he should use tool number

    A. 18　　B. 26　　C. 43　　D. 44

16. If a mechanic is erecting two structural steel plates and needs to line up the bolt holes, he should use tool number

    A. 2　　B. 3　　C. 33　　D. 42

17. To cut reinforcing wire mesh to be used in a concrete floor, you should use tool number

    A. 7　　B. 17　　C. 18　　D. 43

18. The MAIN reason for overhauling a power tool on a regular basis is to

    A. make the men more familiar with the tool
    B. keep the men busy during slack times
    C. insure that the tool is used occasionally
    D. minimize breakdowns

19. A mechanic should NOT press too heavily on a hacksaw while using it to cut through a steel rod because this may

    A. create flying steel particles　　B. bend the frame
    C. break the blade　　D. overheat the rod

20. Creosote is commonly used with wood to

   A. speed-up the seasoning
   B. make the wood fireproof
   C. make painting easier
   D. preserve the wood

21. A mitre box should be used to

   A. hold a saw while sharpening it
   B. store expensive tools
   C. hold a saw at a fixed angle
   D. encase steel beams for protection

22. Wood scaffold planks should be inspected

   A. at regular intervals
   B. before they are stored away
   C. once a week
   D. each time before they are used

23. Continuous sheeting should be used when excavating deep trenches in

   A. rock
   B. stiff clay
   C. firm earth
   D. unstable soil

24. The MAIN reason for requiring that certain special tools be returned to the tool room after a job has been completed is that

   A. missing tools can be replaced
   B. the men will not need to care for the tools
   C. more tools will be available for use
   D. this permits easier inspection and maintenance of tools

25. The BEST material to use to extinguish an oil fire is

   A. sand
   B. water
   C. sawdust
   D. stone gravel

26. A *lally* column is

   A. fabricated from angles and plates
   B. fabricated by tying two channels together with lattice bars
   C. a steel member that has unequal sections
   D. a pipe fitted with a base plate at each end

27. The BEST action for you to take if you discover a small puddle of oil on the shop floor is to FIRST

   A. have it cleaned up
   B. find out who spilled it
   C. discover the source of the leak
   D. cover it with newspaper

28. You should listen to your foreman even when he insists on explaining the procedure for a job you have done many times before because

    A. you can do the job the way you want when he leaves
    B. he may make an error and you can show that you know your job
    C. it is wise to humor him even if he is wrong
    D. you are required to do the job the way the foreman wants it

28.____

Questions 29-34.

DIRECTIONS: Questions 29 through 34 refer to the sketches shown to the right of each question.

29. The indicated pressure is MOST NEARLY _____ psi.
    A. 132
    B. 137
    C. 143
    D. 148

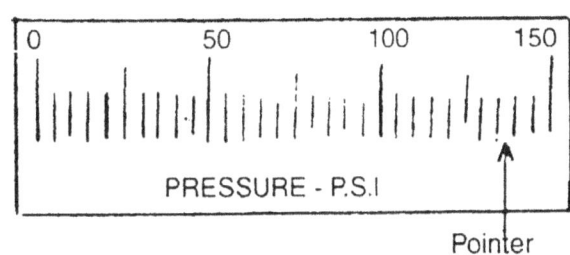

29.____

30. The fewest number of shims, of any combination of thicknesses, required to exactly fill the 1/4" gap shown is
    A. 7
    B. 8
    C. 9
    D. 10

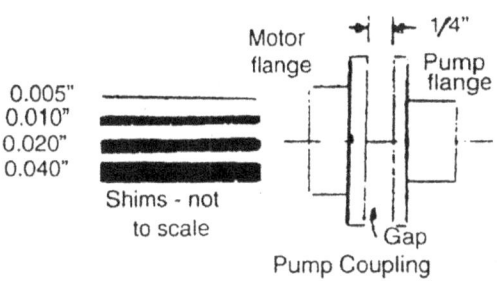

30.____

31. The dimension X on the keyway shown is
    A. 3 3/8"
    B. 3 9/16"
    C. 3 3/4"
    D. 4"

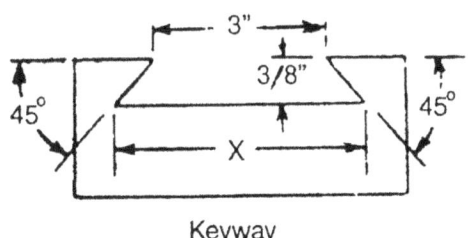

31.____

32. If the tank gage reads 120 psi, then the pipe gage should read _____ psi.
    A. 80
    B. 120
    C. 180
    D. 240

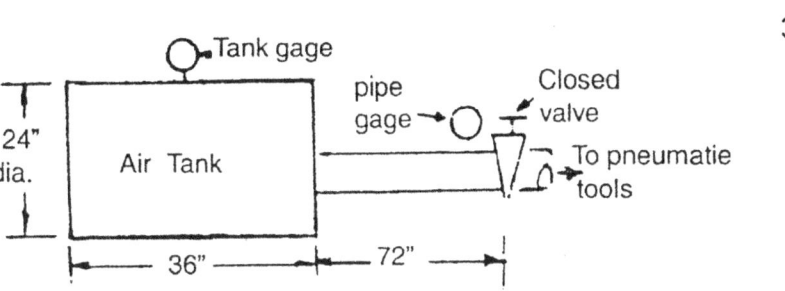

32.____

6 (#1)

33. The MINIMUM number of feet of chainlink fence needed to completely enclose the storage yard shown is
    A. 278
    B. 286
    C. 295
    D. 304

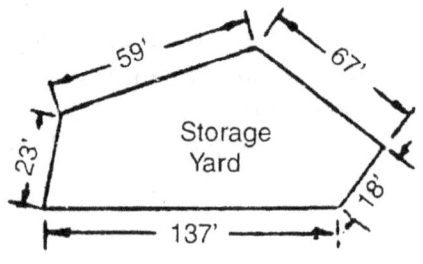

34. The distance X between the holes is
    A. 1 7/8"
    B. 2 1/16"
    C. 2 3/8"
    D. 2 9/16"

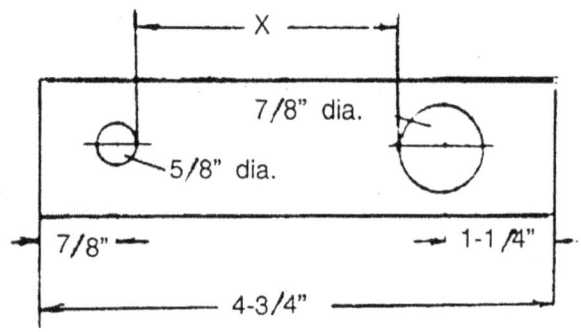

35. A rule of the Transit Authority is that all employees are required to report defective equipment to their superiors, even when the maintenance of the particular equipment is handled by someone else.
    The MAIN purpose of this rule is to
    A. determine who is doing his job improperly
    B. have repairs made before trouble occurs
    C. encourage all employees to be alert at all times
    D. reduce the cost of equipment

36. Some equipment is fitted with wing nuts.
    Such nuts are especially useful when
    A. the nut is to be wired closed
    B. space is limited
    C. the equipment is subject to vibration
    D. the nuts must be removed frequently

37. It is considered bad practice to use water to put out electrical fires MAINLY because the water may
    A. rust the equipment
    B. short circuit the lines
    C. cause a serious shock
    D. damage the electrical insulation

38. While you are being trained, you will be assigned to work with an experienced mechanic.
    It would be BEST for you to
    A. remind the mechanic that he is responsible for your training
    B. tell him frequently how much you know about the work
    C. let him do all the work while you observe closely
    D. be as cooperative and helpful as you can

39. The BEST instrument to use to make certain that two points, separated by a vertical distance of 9 feet, are in perfect vertical alignment is a   39.____

   A. square   B. level   C. plumb bob   D. protractor

40. If a measurement scaled from a drawing is one inch, and the scale of the drawing is 1/8-inch to the foot, then the one inch measurement would represent an actual length of   40.____

   A. 8 feet
   C. 1/8 of a foot
   B. 2 feet
   D. 8 inches

KEY (CORRECT ANSWERS)

1. B	11. B	21. C	31. C
2. B	12. B	22. D	32. B
3. A	13. B	23. D	33. D
4. B	14. C	24. D	34. A
5. B	15. D	25. A	35. B
6. C	16. A	26. D	36. D
7. D	17. D	27. A	37. C
8. D	18. D	28. D	38. D
9. B	19. C	29. B	39. C
10. C	20. D	30. A	40. A

TEST 2

DIRECTIONS: Each question or incomplete statement is followed by several suggested answers or completions. Select the one that BEST answers the question or completes the statement. *PRINT THE LETTER OF THE CORRECT ANSWER IN THE SPACE AT THE RIGHT.*

1. Cloth tapes should NOT be used when accurate measurements must be obtained because

    A. the numbers soon become worn and thus difficult to read
    B. there are not enough subdivisions of each inch on the tape
    C. the ink runs when wet, thus making the tape difficult to read
    D. small changes in the pull on the tape will make considerable differences in tape readings

    1._____

2. It is considered good practice to release the pressure from an air hose before uncoupling the hose connection because this avoids

    A. wasting air
    B. possible personal injury
    C. damage to the air tool
    D. damage to the air compressor

    2._____

3. In brick construction, a structural steel member is used to support the wall above door and window openings. This member is called a

    A. purlin   B. sill   C. truss   D. lintel

    3._____

Questions 4-9.

DIRECTIONS: Questions 4 through 9 show the top view of an object in the first column, the front view of the same object in the second column and four drawings in the third column, one of which correctly represents the RIGHT side view of the object. Select the CORRECT right side view. As a guide, the first one is an illustrative example, the CORRECT answer of which is C.

Questions 10-14.

DIRECTIONS: Questions 10 through 14 are to be answered on the basis of the information contained in the safety regulations given below. In answering these questions, refer to these rules.

REGULATIONS FOR SMALL GROUPS WHO MOVE FROM POINT TO POINT ON THE TRACKS

Employees who perform duties on the tracks in small groups and who move from point to point along the trainway must be on the alert at all times and prepared to clear the track when a train approaches without unnecessarily slowing it down. Underground at all times, and out-of-doors between sunset and sunrise, such employees must not enter upon the tracks unless each of them is equipped with an approved light. Flashlights must not be used for protection by such groups. Upon clearing the track to permit a train to pass, each member of the group must give a proceed signal, by hand or light, to the motorman of the train. Whenever such small groups are working in an area protected by caution lights or flags, but are not members of the gang for whom the flagging protection was established, they must not give proceed signals to motormen. The purpose of this rule is to avoid a motorman's confusing such signal with that of the flagman who is protecting a gang. Whenever a small group is engaged in work of an engrossing nature or at any time when the view of approaching trains is limited by reason of curves or otherwise, one man of the group, equipped with a whistle, must be assigned properly to warn and protect the man or men at work and must not perform any other duties while so assigned.

10. If a small group of men are traveling along the tracks toward their work location and a train approaches, they should

    A. stop the train
    B. signal the motorman to go slowly
    C. clear the track
    D. stop immediately

11. Small groups may enter upon the tracks

    A. only between sunset and sunrise
    B. provided each has an approved light
    C. provided their foreman has a good flashlight
    D. provided each man has an approved flashlight

12. After a small group has cleared the tracks in an area unprotected by caution lights or flags,

    A. each member must give the proceed signal to the motorman
    B. the foreman signals the motorman to proceed
    C. the motorman can proceed provided he goes slowly
    D. the last member off the tracks gives the signal to the motorman

13. If a small group is working in an area protected by the signals of a track gang, the members of the small group

    A. need not be concerned with train movement
    B. must give the proceed signal together with the track gang

C. can delegate one of their members to give the proceed signal
D. must not give the proceed signal

14. If the view of approaching trains is blocked, the small group should

    A. move to where they can see the trains
    B. delegate one of the group to warn and protect them
    C. keep their ears alert for approaching trains
    D. refuse to work at such locations

14.____

15. The information in an accident report which may be MOST useful in helping to prevent similar-type accidents from happening is the

    A. cause of the accident
    B. time of day it happened
    C. type of injuries suffered
    D. number of people injured

15.____

16. The MAIN reason why each coat of paint should be of a different color when two coats of paint are specified is that

    A. cheaper paint can be used as the undercoat
    B. less care need be taken in applying the coats
    C. any missed areas will be easier to spot
    D. the colors do not have to be exact

16.____

Questions 17-23.

DIRECTIONS: Questions 17 through 23 refer to the sketches shown to the right of each question.

17. The distance y is
    A. 5/8"
    B. 7/8"
    C. 1 1/8"
    D. 1 3/8"

17.____

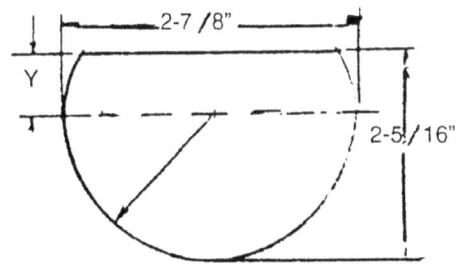

18. The sketch shows the float-operated trippers for operating a sump pump. If you want the pump to start sooner, you should _____ tripper.
    A. *lower* the upper
    B. *lower* the lower
    C. *raise* the upper
    D. *raise* the lower

18.____

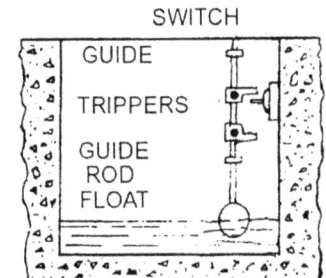

19. The width of the wood stud shown is
    A. 1 1/8"
    B. 1 5/16"
    C. 1 5/8"
    D. 3 5/8"

19. ___

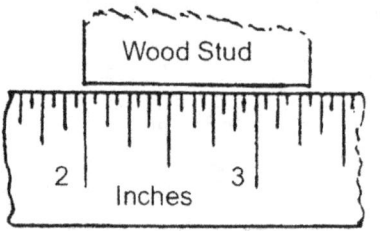

20. The right angle shown has been divided into four unequal parts.
    The number of degrees in angle X is
    A. 31°
    B. 33°
    C. 38°
    D. 45°

20. ___

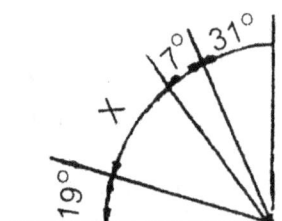

21. The reading on the meter shown is MOST NEARLY
    A. 0465
    B. 0475
    C. 0566
    D. 1566

21. ___

22. The length X of the slot shown is
    A. 2 3/8"
    B. 2 7/16"
    C. 2 1/2"
    D. 2 9/16"

22. ___

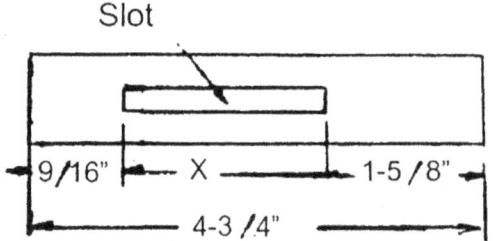

23. The volume of the bar shown is _____ cubic inches.
    A. 132
    B. 356
    C. 420
    D. 516

23. ___

24. Gaskets should be used with

    A. flanged pipe fittings
    C. threaded reducing couplings
    B. bell and spigot pipe
    D. threaded bushings

24. ___

25. The MAIN purpose for providing a plumbing fixture with a trap is to

    A. equalize the pressures in the drainage system
    B. catch any article that might plug the drain
    C. prevent passage of gases
    D. supply an easy means of cleaning if the fixture gets plugged

26. The *soil stack* of a drainage system is left open at its upper end in order to

    A. prevent the sewer from backing up into the traps
    B. prevent the siphoning of traps
    C. prevent ventilation of the drainage system
    D. hold a vacuum above the house drain line

27. Under the city color coding of pipes, drinking water pipes should be painted

    A. blue B. yellow C. green D. red

28. When changing from a 2" pipe size to a 1" pipe in a horizontal steam line, the PROPER fitting to be used is a(n)

    A. concentric bushing
    B. face bushing
    C. concentric reducer
    D. eccentric reducer

29. An expansion slip joint

    A. permits longitudinal movement of a pipe
    B. is used when the pipe has been cut short
    C. compensates for differences in pipe pressure
    D. permits small movement for lining pipe hangers

30. The MAIN reason why brass is better than iron for water piping is that brass is

    A. cheaper
    B. lighter
    C. stronger
    D. more corrosion resistant

31. A bell and spigot cast iron pipe joint is made water-tight by

    A. rolling and beading the ends
    B. caulking with oakum and lead
    C. caulking with cotton wick and cement
    D. applying sealing compound to the threaded ends

32. The one of the following valves which is ALWAYS automatic in operation is the _____ valve.

    A. gate B. angle C. check D. globe

33. Threaded joints may be made up tight by using pipe thread compound. The CORRECT procedure is to apply the compound

    A. only to the male threads
    B. only to the female threads
    C. to both male and female threads
    D. to either the male or female thread, depending on the pipe size

Questions 34-39.

DIRECTIONS: Questions 34 through 39 are to be answered on the basis of the riser diagram shown below.

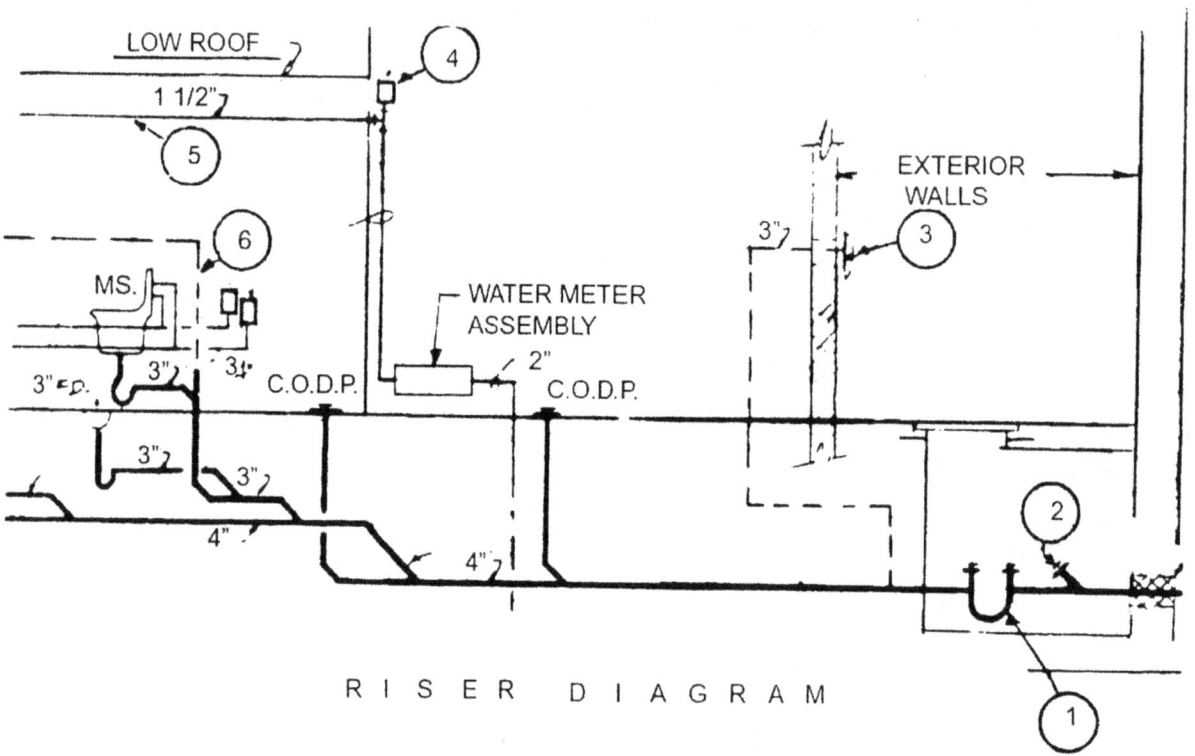

RISER DIAGRAM

34. Fitting 1 is a

    A. floor drain   B. trap
    C. clean out   D. check valve

35. Fitting 2 is a

    A. floor drain   B. trap
    C. clean out   D. check valve

36. Fitting 3 is a

    A. fire department connection
    B. sprinkler head
    C. valve
    D. fresh air inlet

37. Fitting 4 is a(n)

    A. gate valve   B. air chamber
    C. running trap   D. vent inlet

38. Line 5 is a

    A. hot water pipe
    B. vent line
    C. cold water line
    D. soil line

39. Line 6 is a _____ line.

    A. vent
    B. cold water
    C. hot water
    D. drain

40. A non-rising stem-type gate valve is especially useful when

    A. the stem must move downward only
    B. the pressure in the pipe must remain constant
    C. clearances around the valve are limited
    D. hand control of the valve is not required

KEY (CORRECT ANSWERS)

1. D	11. B	21. A	31. B
2. B	12. A	22. D	32. C
3. D	13. D	23. C	33. A
4. C	14. B	24. A	34. B
5. A	15. A	25. C	35. C
6. C	16. C	26. B	36. D
7. B	17. B	27. C	37. B
8. B	18. D	28. D	38. C
9. C	19. B	29. A	39. A
10. C	20. B	30. D	40. C

EXAMINATION SECTION

TEST 1

DIRECTIONS: In each of the following questions, only one of the four sentences conforms to standards of correct usage. The other three contain errors in grammar, diction, or punctuation. Select the choice in each question which BEST conforms to standards of correct usage. Consider a choice correct if it contains none of the errors mentioned above, even though there may be other ways of expressing the same thought. *PRINT THE LETTER OF THE CORRECT ANSWER IN THE SPACE AT THE RIGHT.*

1. A. Because he was ill was no excuse for his behavior
   B. I insist that he see a lawyer before he goes to trial.
   C. He said "that he had not intended to go."
   D. He wasn't out of the office only three days.

   1.____

2. A. He came to the station and pays a porter to carry his bags into the train.
   B. I should have liked to live in medieval times.
   C. My father was born in Linville. A little country town where everybody knows everyone else.
   D. The car, which is parked across the street, is disabled.

   2.____

3. A. He asked the desk clerk for a clean, quiet, room.
   B. I expected James to be lonesome and that he would want to go home.
   C. I have stopped worrying because I have heard nothing further on the subject.
   D. If the board of directors controls the company, they may take actions which are disapproved by the stockholders.

   3.____

4. A. Each of the players knew their place.
   B. He whom you saw on the stage is the son of an actor.
   C. Susan is the smartest of the twin sisters.
   D. Who ever thought of him winning both prizes?

   4.____

5. A. An outstanding trait of early man was their reliance on omens.
   B. Because I had never been there before.
   C. Neither Mr. Jones nor Mr. Smith has completed his work.
   D. While eating my dinner, a dog came to the window.

   5.____

6. A. A copy of the lease, in addition to the Rules and Regulations, are to be given to each tenant.
   B. The Rules and Regulations and a copy of the lease is being given to each tenant.
   C. A copy of the lease, in addition to the Rules and Regulations, is to be given to each tenant.
   D. A copy of the lease, in addition to the Rules and Regulations, are being given to each tenant.

   6.____

7. A. Although we understood that for him music was a passion, we were disturbed   7.____
       by the fact that he was addicted to sing along with the soloists.
    B. Do you believe that Steven is liable to win a scholarship?
    C. Give the picture to whomever is a connoisseur of art.
    D. Whom do you believe to be the most efficient worker in the office?

8. A. Each adult who is sure they know all the answers will some day realize   8.____
       their mistake.
    B. Even the most hardhearted villain would have to feel bad about so horrible
       a tragedy.
    C. Neither being licensed teachers, both aspirants had to pass rigorous tests
       before being appointed.
    D. The principal reason why he wanted to be designated was because he had
       never before been to a convention.

9. A. Being that the weather was so inclement, the party has been postponed for   9.____
       at least a month.
    B. He is in New York City only three weeks and he has already seen all the
       thrilling sights in Manhattan and in the other four boroughs.
    C. If you will look it up in the official directory, which can be consulted in the
       library during specified hours, you will discover that the chairman and
       director are Mr. T. Henry Long.
    D. Working hard at college during the day and at the post office during the
       night, he appeared to his family to be indefatigable.

10. A. I would have been happy to oblige you if you only asked me to do it.   10.____
    B. The cold weather, as well as the unceasing wind and rain, have made us
       decide to spend the winter in Florida.
    C. The politician would have been more successful in winning office if he
       would have been less dogmatic.
    D. These trousers are expensive; however, they will wear well.

11. A. All except him wore formal attire at the reception for the ambassador.   11.____
    B. If that chair were to be blown off of the balcony, it might injure someone
       below.
    C. Not a passenger, who was in the crash, survived the impact.
    D. To borrow money off friends is the best way to lose them.

12. A. Approaching Manhattan on the ferry boat from Staten Island, an   12.____
       unforgettable sight of the skyscrapers is seen.
    B. Did you see the exhibit of modernistic paintings as yet?
    C. Gesticulating wildly and ranting in stentorian tones, the speaker was the
       sinecure of all eyes.
    D. The airplane with crew and passengers was lost somewhere in the Pacific
       Ocean.

3 (#1)

13.
   A. If one has consistently had that kind of training, it is certainly too late to change your entire method of swimming long distances.
   B. The captain would have been more impressed if you would have been more conscientious in evacuation drills.
   C. The passengers on the stricken ship were all ready to abandon it at the signal.
   D. The villainous shark lashed at the lifeboat with it's tail, trying to upset the rocking boat in order to partake of it's contents.

13.____

14.
   A. As one whose been certified as a professional engineer, I believe that the decision to build a bridge over that harbor is unsound.
   B. Between you and me, this project ought to be completed long before winter arrives.
   C. He fervently hoped that the men would be back at camp and to find them busy at their usual chores.
   D. Much to his surprise, he discovered that the climate of Korea was like his home town.

14.____

15.
   A. An industrious executive is aided, not impeded, by having a hobby which gives him a fresh point of view on life and its problems.
   B. Frequent absence during the calendar year will surely mitigate against the chances of promotion.
   C. He was unable to go to the committee meeting because he was very ill.
   D. Mr. Brown expressed his disapproval so emphatically that his associates were embarassed

15.____

16.
   A. At our next session, the office manager will have told you something about his duties and responsibilities.
   B. In general, the book is absorbing and original and have no hesitation about recommending it.
   C. The procedures followed by private industry in dealing with lateness and absence are different from ours.
   D We shall treat confidentially any information about Mr. Doe, to whom we understand you have sent reports to for many years.

16.____

17.
   A. I talked to one official, whom I knew was fully impartial.
   B. Everyone signed the petition but him.
   C. He proved not only to be a good student but also a good athlete.
   D. All are incorrect.

17.____

18.
   A. Every year a large amount of tenants are admitted to housing projects.
   B. Henry Ford owned around a billion dollars in industrial equipment.
   C. He was aggravated by the child's poor behavior.
   D. All are incorrect.

18.____

19. A. Before he was committed to the asylum he suffered from the illusion that he was Napoleon.
    B. Besides stocks, there were also bonds in the safe.
    C. We bet the other team easily.
    D. All are incorrect.

    19.____

20. A. Bring this report to your supervisory.
    B. He set the chair down near the table.
    C. The capitol of New York is Albany.
    D. All are incorrect.

    20.____

21. A. He was chosen to arbitrate the dispute because everyone knew he would be disinterested.
    B. It is advisable to obtain the best council before making an important decision.
    C. Less college students are interested in teaching than ever before.
    D. All are incorrect.

    21.____

22. A. She, hearing a signal, the source lamp flashed.
    B. While hearing a signal, the source lamp flashed.
    C. In hearing a signal, the source lamp flashed.
    D. As she heard a signal, the source lamp flashed.

    22.____

23. A. Every one of the time records have been initialed in the designated spaces.
    B. All of the time records has been initialed in the designated spaces.
    C. Each one of the time records was initialed in the designated spaces.
    D. The time records all been initialed in the designated spaces.

    23.____

24. A. If there is no one else to answer the phone, you will have to answer it.
    B. You will have to answer it yourself if no one else answers the phone.
    C. If no one else is not around to pick up the phone, you will have to do it.
    D. You will have to answer the phone when nobodys here to do it.

    24.____

25. A. Dr. Barnes not in his office. What could I do for you?
    B. Dr. Barnes is not in his office. Is there something I can do for you?
    C. Since Dr. Barnes is not in his office, might there be something I may do for you?
    D. Is there any ways I can assist you since Dr. Barnes is not in his office?

    25.____

26. A. She do not understand how the new console works.
    B. The way the new console works, she doesn't understand.
    C. She doesn't understand how the new console works.
    D. The new console works, so that she doesn't understand.

    26.____

27. A. Certain changes in my family income must be reported as they occur.
    B. When certain changes in family income occur, it must be reported.
    C. Certain family income change must be reported as they occur.
    D. Certain changes in family income must be reported as they have been occurring.

    27.____

28. A. Each tenant has to complete the application themselves.
     B. Each of the tenants have to complete the application by himself.
     C. Each of the tenants has to complete the application himself.
     D. Each of the tenants has to complete the application by themselves.

28._____

29. A. Yours is the only building that the construction will effect.
     B. Your's is the only building affected by the construction.
     C. The construction will only effect your building.
     D. Yours is the only building that will be affected by the construction.

29._____

30. A. There is four tests left.
     B. The number of tests left are four.
     C. There are four tests left.
     D. Four of the tests remains.

30._____

31. A. Each of the applicants takes a test.
     B. Each of the applicant take a test.
     C. Each of the applicants take tests.
     D. Each of the applicants have taken tests.

31._____

32. A. The applicant, not the examiners, are ready.
     B. The applicants, not the examiners, is ready.
     C. The applicants, not the examiner, are ready.
     D. The applicant, not the examiner, are ready

32._____

33. A. You will not progress except you practice.
     B. You will not progress without you practicing.
     C. You will not progress unless you practice.
     D. You will not progress provided you do not practice.

33._____

34. A. Neither the director or the employees will be at the office tomorrow.
     B. Neither the director nor the employees will be at the office tomorrow.
     C. Neither the director, or the secretary nor the other employees will be at the office tomorrow.
     D. Neither the director, the secretary or the other employees will be at the office tomorrow.

34._____

35. A. In my absence, he and her will have to finish the assignment.
     B. In my absence he and she will have to finish the assignment.
     C. In my absence she and him, they will have to finish the assignment.
     D. In my absence he and her both will have to finish the assignment.

35._____

KEY (CORRECT ANSWERS)

1.	B	11.	A	21.	A	31.	A
2.	B	12.	D	22.	D	32.	C
3.	C	13.	C	23.	C	33.	C
4.	B	14.	B	24.	A	34.	B
5.	C	15.	A	25.	B	35.	B
6.	C	16.	C	26.	C		
7.	D	17.	B	27.	A		
8.	B	18.	D	28.	C		
9.	D	19.	B	29.	D		
10.	D	20.	B	30.	C		

TEST 2

DIRECTIONS: Each question or incomplete statement is followed by several suggested answers or completions. Select the one that BEST answers the question or completes the statement. *PRINT THE LETTER OF THE CORRECT ANSWER IN THE SPACE AT THE RIGHT.*

Questions 1-4.

DIRECTIONS: Questions 1 through 4 consist of three sentences each. For each question, select the sentence which contains NO error in grammar or usage.

1. A. Be sure that everybody brings his notes to the conference. 1.____
   B. He looked like he meant to hit the boy.
   C. Mr. Jones is one of the clients who was chosen to represent the district.
   D. All are incorrect.

2. A. He is taller than I. 2.____
   B. I'll have nothing to do with these kind of people.
   C. The reason why he will not buy the house is because it is too expensive.
   D. All are incorrect.

3. A. Aren't I eligible for this apartment. 3.____
   B. Have you seen him anywheres?
   C. He should of come earlier.
   D. All are incorrect.

4. A. He graduated college in 2022. 4.____
   B. He hadn't but one more line to write.
   C. Who do you think is the author of this report?
   D. All are incorrect.

Questions 5-35.

DIRECTIONS: In each of the following questions, only one of the four sentences conforms to standards of correct usage. The other three contain errors in grammar, diction, or punctuation. Select the choice in each question which BEST conforms to standards of correct usage. Consider a choice correct if it contains none of the errors mentioned above, even though there may be other ways of expressing the same thought.

5. A. It is obvious that no one wants to be a kill-joy if they can help it. 5.____
   B. It is not always possible, and perhaps it never ispossible, to judge a person's character by just looking at him.
   C. When Yogi Berra of the New York Yankees hit an immortal grandslam home run, everybody in the huge stadium including Pittsburgh fans, rose to his feet.
   D. Every one of us students must pay tuition today.

6. A. The physician told the young mother that if the baby is not able to digest its milk, it should be boiled.
    B. There is no doubt whatsoever that he felt deeply hurt because John Smith had betrayed the trust.
    C. Having partaken of a most delicious repast prepared by Tessie Breen, the hostess, the horses were driven home immediately thereafter.
    D. The attorney asked my wife and myself several questions.

    6.____

7. A. Despite all denials, there is no doubt in my mind that
    B. At this time everyone must deprecate the demogogic attack made by one of our Senators on one of our most revered statesmen.
    C. In the first game of a crucial two-game series, Ted Williams, got two singles, both of them driving in a run.
    D. Our visitor brought good news to John and I.

    7.____

8. A. If he would have told me, I should have been glad to help him in his dire financial emergency.
    B. Newspaper men have often asserted that diplomats or so-called official spokesmen sometimes employ equivocation in attempts to deceive.
    C. I think someones coming to collect money for the Red Cross.
    D. In a masterly summation, the young attorney expressed his belief that the facts clearly militate against this opinion.

    8.____

9. A. We have seen most all the exhibits.
    B. Without in the least underestimating your advice, in my opinion the situation has grown immeasurably worse in the past few days.
    C. I wrote to the box office treasurer of the hit show that a pair of orchestra seats would be preferable.
    D. As the grim story of Pearl Harbor was broadcast on that fateful December 7, it was the general opinion that war was inevitable.

    9.____

10. A. Without a moment's hesitation, Casey Stengel said that Larry Berra works harder than any player on the team.
    B. There is ample evidence to indicate that many animals can run faster than any human being.
    C. No one saw the accident but I.
    D. Example of courage is the heroic defense put up by the paratroopers against overwhelming odds.

    10.____

11. A. If you prefer these kind, Mrs. Grey, we shall be more than willing to let you have them reasonably.
    B. If you like these here, Mrs. Grey, we shall be more than willing to let you have them reasonably.
    C. If you like these, Mrs. Grey, we shall be more than willing to let you have them.
    D. Who shall we appoint?

    11.____

12.
    A. The number of errors are greater in speech than in writing.
    B. The doctor rather than the nurse was to blame for his being neglected.
    C. Because the demand for these books have been so great, we reduced the price.
    D. John Galsworthy, the English novelist, could not have survived a serious illness; had it not been for loving care.

    12.____

13.
    A. Our activities this year have seldom ever been as interesting as they have been this month.
    B. Our activities this month have been more interesting, or at least as interesting as those of any month this year.
    C. Our activities this month has been more interesting than those of any other month this year.
    D. Neither Jean nor her sister was at home.

    13.____

14.
    A. George B. Shaw's view of common morality, as well as his wit sparkling with a dash of perverse humor here and there, have led critics to term him "The Incurable Rebel."
    B. The President's program was not always received with the wholehearted endorsement of his own party, which is why the party faces difficulty in drawing up a platform for the coming election.
    C. The reason why they wanted to travel was because they had never been away from home.
    D. Facing a barrage of cameras, the visiting celebrity found it extremely difficult to express his opinions clearly.

    14.____

15.
    A. When we calmed down, we all agreed that our anger had been kind of unnecessary and had not helped the situation.
    B. Without him going into all the details, he made us realize the horror of the accident.
    C. Like one girl, for example, who applied for two positions.
    D. Do not think that you have to be so talented as he is in order to play in the school orchestra.

    15.____

16.
    A. He looked very peculiarly to me.
    B. He certainly looked at me peculiar.
    C. Due to the train's being late, we had to wait an hour.
    D. The reason for the poor attendance is that it is raining.

    16.____

17.
    A. About one out of four own an automobile.
    B. The collapse of the old Mitchell Bridge was caused by defective construction in the central pier.
    C. Brooks Atkinson was well acquainted with the best literature, thus helping him to become an able critic.
    D. He has to stand still until the relief man comes up, thus giving him no chance to move about and keep warm.

    17.____

18. A. He is sensitive to confusion and withdraws from people whom he feels are too noisy.
     B. Do you know whether the data is statistically correct?
     C. Neither the mayor or the aldermen are to blame.
     D. Of those who were graduated from high school, a goodly percentage went to college.

19. A. Acting on orders, the offices were searched by a designated committee.
     B. The answer probably is nothing.
     C. I thought it to be all right to excuse them from class.
     D. I think that he is as successful a singer, if not more successful, than Mary.

20. A. $360,000 is really very little to pay for such a wellbuilt house.
     B. The creatures looked like they had come from outer space.
     C. It was her, he knew!
     D. Nobody but me knows what to do.

21. A. Mrs. Smith looked good in her new suit.
     B. New York may be compared with Chicago.
     C. I will not go to the meeting except you go with me.
     D. I agree with this editorial.

22. A. My opinions are different from his.
     B. There will be less students in class now.
     C. Helen was real glad to find her watch.
     D. It had been pushed off of her dresser.

23. A. Almost everyone, who has been to California, returns with glowing reports.
     B. George Washington, John Adams, and Thomas Jefferson, were our first presidents.
     C. Mr. Walters, whom we met at the bank yesterday, is the man, who gave me my first job.
     D. One should study his lessons as carefully as he can.

24. A. We had such a good time yesterday.
     B. When the bell rang, the boys and girls went in the schoolhouse.
     C. John had the worst headache when he got up this morning.
     D. Today's assignment is somewhat longer than yesterday's.

25. A. Neither the mayor nor the city clerk are willing to talk.
     B. Neither the mayor nor the city clerk is willing to talk.
     C. Neither the mayor or the city clerk are willing to talk.
     D Neither the mayor or the city clerk is willing to talk.

26. A. Being that he is that kind of boy, cooperation cannot be expected.
     B. He interviewed people who he thought had something to say.
     C. Stop whomever enters the building regardless of rank or office held.
     D. Passing through the countryside, the scenery pleased us.

27. A. The childrens' shoes were in their closet.
     B. The children's shoes were in their closet.
     C. The childs' shoes were in their closet.
     D. The childs' shoes were in his closet.

28. A. An agreement was reached between the defendant, the plaintiff, the plaintiff's attorney and the insurance company as to the amount of the settlement.
     B. Everybody was asked to give their versions of the accident.
     C. The consensus of opinion was that the evidence was inconclusive.
     D. The witness stated that if he was rich, he wouldn't have had to loan the money.

29. A. Before beginning the investigation, all the materials related to the case were carefully assembled.
     B. The reason for his inability to keep the appointment is because of his injury in the accident.
     C. This here evidence tends to support the claim of the defendant.
     D. We interviewed all the witnesses who, according to the driver, were still in town.

30. A. Each claimant was allowed the full amount of their medical expenses.
     B. Either of the three witnesses is available.
     C. Every one of the witnesses was asked to tell his story.
     D. Neither of the witnesses are right.

31. A. The commissioner, as well as his deputy and various bureau heads, were present.
     B. A new organization of employers and employees have been formed.
     C. One or the other of these men have been selected.
     D. The number of pages in the book is enough to discourage a reader.

32. A. Between you and me, I think he is the better man.
     B. He was believed to be me.
     C. Is it us that you wish to see?
     D. The winners are him and her.

33. A. Beside the statement to the police, the witness spoke to no one.
     B. He made no statement other than to the police and I.
     C. He made no statement to any one else, aside from the police.
     D. The witness spoke to no one but me.

34. A. The claimant has no one to blame but himself.
     B. The boss sent us, he and I, to deliver the packages.
     C. The lights come from mine and not his car.
     D. There was room on the stairs for him and myself.

35. A. Admission to this clinic is limited to patients' inability to pay for medical care.
     B. Patients who can pay little or nothing for medical care are treated in this clinic.
     C. The patient's ability to pay for medical care is the determining factor in his admission to this clinic.
     D. This clinic is for the patient's that cannot afford to pay or that can pay a little for medical care.

35.____

KEY (CORRECT ANSWERS)

1.	A	11.	C	21.	A	31.	D
2.	A	12.	B	22.	A	32.	A
3.	D	13.	D	23.	D	33.	D
4.	C	14.	D	24.	D	34.	A
5.	D	15.	D	25.	B	35.	B
6.	D	16.	D	26.	B		
7.	B	17.	B	27.	B		
8.	B	18.	D	28.	C		
9.	D	19.	B	29.	D		
10.	B	20.	D	30.	C		

www.ingramcontent.com/pod-product-compliance
Lightning Source LLC
Chambersburg PA
CBHW080322020526
44117CB00035B/2599